So You Think You're a Good Citizen

Walter W. Lamb

ikon publishing

Ikon Publishing
www.ikonpublishing.ca

Lamb, Walter W.
So You Think You're a Good Citizen / Walter W. Lamb

ISBN 0-9735825-3-7

Hard Cover Edition

Cover & text design: Ariel Janzen

This Book is Dedicated To

My father who saw that I received a proper education

My mother who was a teacher until fate dealt her a bad hand

My wife, Rusty, who has a knack of bringing out the best in me

And our children, Doug, Charlie, Gar, Kevin and Sandy,
all of whom I hope succeed in achieving their goals in life

And was completed with the assistance of

My editor, Owen Lock, whose wit, stories,
and technical support made it happen.

AND

Jeff Wallace, Editor, Aiken Standard;
Andy Reeves, Aiken County School District Superintendant;
Nancy Lex, Aiken High School Librarian;
Janet L. Robinson, Aiken Regional Public Reference Librarian;
Bob Rogers, neighbor Audrey, Gen. Joe Franklin and
Miles Hall, who kept me on the correct path.

Contents

Foreword

Normally, we consider being a good citizen means: being considerate of others, obeying the laws, going to church on a frequent basis, voting, and being aware of the issues. Is that enough?

As I witness events in the world around us, I appreciate being a citizen of these United States more and more. We take freedoms for granted that others in the world hope, pray, even die for.

When I was a substitute teacher, it seemed to me that our young people needed a wake-up call about just how our government process works. In fact, given a national percentage of no-shows at the polls that hovers around 50%, it may be that we all need a reminder of the issues before us.

The results of inattention to any single issue discussed in this book will not cause our country to fail, but the direction in which we are headed, the apathy of the electorate, and the slow erosion of our liberties all give me concern about our future.

We must become better informed about how the mechanisms of our nation work, be aware of any issues that might weaken the family, and educate our younger generations as to what is at stake: our way of life.

My challenge, to each of you, is to investigate the truth about the issues discussed here, and others that you may identify as extremely important, and then to let your representative know your thoughts, in detail and with footnotes. Keep your head high, get involved, and make a difference in your life. It is not too late…yet.

Walter W. Lamb
Aiken, South Carolina
31 July 2004

Chapter One

The Freedom that Education Provides

The preservation of liberty depends upon the intellectual and moral character of the people. As long as knowledge and virtue are diffused generally among the body of a nation, it is impossible they should be enslaved.

John Adams

All of us have parents, but not all are so fortunate as to have had their complete attention and to have had them immediately available throughout our developing years. A tip of the hat to those parents who remained around, because they are the ones who give us hope for the future of the nation.

Education, in the broadest sense, is a continuing, unending, process, and the family, whether it has one parent or two, is the bedrock of a strong nation. The "family" either supports an effective education or goes along with the system. In the latter case, fortunately, our system sometime graduates strong leaders because the student is inspired by a role model. Participation in sports activities teaches children to recognize there are rules and that we indeed have choices. In the process of education we develop an understanding of what is right and wrong and the bounds of acceptable behavior.

When parents are largely or wholly absent from the educational process gangs form. Money, drugs, power, the normal childish reaction to the imposition of authority, and a "something for nothing" attitude, influence the formation of gangs. Corrupt government officials and poor leadership fan the embers of unrest that normally glow within the chests of the young, and they create a desire for a strong "family". The basic, down to bedrock answer to the formation of gangs and the attitudes that accompany them is a strong family unit. Where gangs form they are the substitute family.

We must not stray from support of the family unit. We must be vigilant in the quest to keep the basic principles which rule society clear and above question. Is it really easy to understand the effect of handouts to the family, instead of working for the right to make their own choices? Each of us wants to help our neighbor who is not as fortunate, but what is the long-term solution?

When I lived in Houston, Texas, I had the good luck to be exposed to the Knowledge Is Power Program (KIPP). Started by teachers Mike Feinberg and Dave Levin in 1994, the program expanded from 50 fifth graders in the inner city to two KIPP schools: KIPP Academy Houston and KIPP Academy New York.

The performance of the program has been impressive: ninety-nine percent of its students matriculate into high schools, and its students have earned more than 18 million dollars in scholarships. The fall of 2003 saw the program's first alumni enter college. KIPP's successes have attracted support. To date, KIPP has grown into a national network of 31 schools in thirteen states and the District of Columbia.

Among other things, KIPP requires parents of participating students to sign off on the total program. The sorely-needed commitment of the family is there, but KIPP is a private/public system that avoids problems brought on by mediocre teaching. It eliminates the problem of poor discipline by marrying authority and responsibility. Can the same thing be done on a large scale in public school systems? Not just yet; that would require a very large amount of work by our politicians and it cannot be successfully implemented merely by allocating sufficient funds.

We would have to rework the legal system in order to return control of children to their parents. Further, the parents would have to allow teachers to discipline students without fear of legal retaliation because responsibility and authority must be in balance.[1]

Our forefathers liked the idea of letting state government experiment with new programs before they became federal in scope. We have a system here, The KIPP system, which warrants major scrutiny because, if it can be put into widespread use, the nation will reap great rewards. So I propose that we develop a national test program, one that is to be voted on via a referendum and implemented by the three states which have the highest proportion of their citizens voting in the program's favor. Those three states would become the testing ground. If we cannot install a system such as that, then we must implement massive reformation of our school system; we will not succeed as a nation if we accept mediocrity as the norm. For more on KIPP, see www.kipp.org.

Not only have the basics of proper education been neglected, but for some reason we have forgotten that the major reason for a

---

[1] We will return to this subject in Chapter Five, "The Keystone of the Republic."

public education is to produce self-supporting citizens. Further, the time has come to accept the fact that not everyone is suited for college and not everyone has the desire to attend college.

Most high schools provide programs for careers that will not require any advanced degree. On average, one can expect 10% of the students in a given school to participate in such programs (cooking, art, automotive and electronics maintenance, shop skills, etc.). The breadth of the programs and the percentage of students participating in them varies from school to school. State-supported "tech" schools and community colleges are also proving to be effective producers of employable young people.

Does a child get more involved in, say, a sport in which she excels or in a subject he can identify with? These are important questions because the sooner students "find" themselves, the faster they become qualified to advance in endeavors they like. History tells us that people not only do better, but like themselves more and are better citizens when they are working in fields they enjoy. Thus, it should be evident that one of the keys to success as an individual is to receive an education in a field one likes, and as soon as possible. Many writers, entertainers, and athletes could be identified in high school because they were doggedly persistent in achieving the goal of being the best at what they did.

First, they found their niche early. Second, they generally had support, whether from the family, a role model, or a mentor. Finally, they had enough drive to carry out their quest for perfection. Life provides many obstacles, but a sound education goes a long way to help one overcome them. A second classroom, at home in the family environment, is a must for excellence.

The family provides the foundation for perseverance. We all stumble now and again, and we need someone to trust in moments of need. Think about it: If you have a job, a family, and money in the bank, life is sweet; if you lose your money, you still have a job and family, you can still see a good future; if you lose your money and your job, you still have your family to nurture you until things are better, you still have your skills but life is difficult; if you lose all three, at the same time, you stand alone. Only your education, and the ability to apply that education, along with determination, will see you through. The government is there for minimal support, and as a last resort.

Through the experience of failure we learn to eliminate unsound ideas. Conversely, we learn to promote those thoughts and procedures that are more efficient. Only governments can afford inefficiency, and even they can fail.[2] Education before college teaches us rudimentary skills, basic knowledge, and where to find information. As time passes, through social interaction, most of us learn how to deal with all kinds of people.

Lets take a peek at the interesting subject of locating information. We have our family, friends, acquaintances, and, perhaps, professionals we know; newspapers, TV, radio, magazines, and books; the library and the Internet. In high school and college, the library, an organized, magnificent mountain of knowledge, is very important.

Today, in addition to the mostly passive resources provided by the library, we have the Internet. That is more of a challenge than ever. Computer programs help us write and spell. We can have income taxes calculated, and submitted, on line! We can communicate with many people, and at little or no expense. We can reconcile the checkbook, even categorize items for personal, business, and tax purposes. Investment assistance is available, based on the size of one's wallet; if you dare, trades can be executed on the Internet as well. And the search engines! Let your fingers do the walking... travel, history, and government info abounds. And buy something? Easily done provided only that you take care to see that your personal data doesn't fall into the wrong hands.

Yes, learning how to use the Internet is an education in itself. But it won't teach you right from wrong, whether the facts that are alleged there are accurate, or even if the pictures you see are real (rather than "Photoshopped"). The Internet is a tool, a powerful

[2] See Chapter Four, "Politics USA Style."

tool, and we must learn both its strengths and its very real limitations. Misinformation and half-truths found there can be very damaging because they are so difficult to pick out. Recently, a test was displayed on the Internet, one that was purportedly given to 8th graders in 1895, In reality the test was for 8th grade *teachers*, who at that time had, on average, eighth-grade educations. A copy of the test appears as Appendix A, at the rear of this book. The examination is quite interesting. I recommend that the reader try it on him- or herself.

After reading Appendix A, we should ask ourselves, what should our 8th graders, or 12th graders, know today? Our society is not as agrarian. We live in the computer age. Even the poorest and most backward nations of the world have recognized the value of the computer.[3] There are jobs "on" the Internet, they are created there, and the kinds of jobs to be made there are limited only by the imagination. And they do not require a college education. Have you received a call from India lately?

Education includes learning how best to use time. The one item we have more choices with, the one thing that demonstrates some of our personality, that gives us insight, is also our window to the world. How big is your window?

By example, the family provides education in the uses of time: when to work, play, cleanup, rest, eat, etc. We have choices: do we accept, run down, or try to improve our experiences? And against what other experiences do we model them?

As we progress through the school systems, we are given more freedom with our time. Whether we like it or not, orderly activity requires training through repetition. The proper use of time becomes more critical as we mature, as we are expected to be "responsible." Do you consciously evaluate how you use your time?

In typical classrooms of the 8th through the 12th grades, one can see the students slowly, but unconsciously absorbing the lesson that disturbances in class do not pay; each year teachers spend less time controlling and more time teaching. Concurrently, the more

---

[3] *Fortune*, 09 February 2004, "Catch Us If You Can."

parental involvement is an aspect of the education, the faster learning becomes an actuality. Smart kids value the education agenda; those who are very smart quickly grow bored and do not keep up; the less smart, take the easy way. Good teachers are alert to the various agendas and must react to each student with the proper tools of control. That is not an easy assignment.

But, have you seen a course in high school that teaches the importance of time, and how to be efficient in its use? Once mastered that is a skill to be applied to every aspect of our lives.

And then there is money. As individuals, if we planned the proper use of our money, the banks would be very unhappy. But make certain that your secondary school, whether public or private, teaches its students how to handle or budget money. A family-taught subject? We may be certain that the bank lobbyists would have well-chosen comments about teaching that subject rigorously in public schools. The family teaches the value of a dollar.

We have this problem: We want our children to have the things we didn't. Thus, money flows in their direction, frequently without too much accountability. Yes: Time and Money, Money and Time, those are important subjects.

For those of you who would like an easy way to introduce family budgeting considerations to your teenagers, some basic comments appear in Appendix B. Those of you who know all about budgeting are spared the necessity of reading it there. However, I do ask you to consider two questions: Who taught you about how to make up and to maintain a family budget? Who is teaching your children how to make up and maintain a family budget?

And then there are priorities. Every family has its own idiosyncrasies, and that is as it should be. Do we educate our children in the complexity of running a family by inviting them into family discussions, or are such things considered "adult" matters because we find the children's comments are not grounded in experience? Is it a practical use of our limited free time to involve the kids? Well, how better to teach our children than to make them aware of the factors and priorities we use in the decision process? Of course it is not practical on a routine basis, but think of the opportunity we have to show them how a parent's mind works. Speaking of being an ideal parent, do we all have role models we admire? Choices....

Why bring up the subjects of time and money? Because those two problems are the major causes of family dissention and turmoil. If we could develop a way to deal with those two monsters, family life would be much more positive. Learning that the first step in solving any problem is properly identifying it is also part of the problem.

On a more positive note, we should think seriously about adding "the use of time and money" to the high school curriculum. Our students need it, we need it, the nation needs it. Education is a life-long process, and it should be initiated and nurtured by the family. To a large extent, a person's progress in life depends upon the individual, but it certainly helps to have a loving family.

Regrettably, if one is not a student of the Bible, one becomes dependent on a minister for better insight on its meaning. And it is truly said that virtually any opinion can be substantiated somewhere in the Bible. The same conclusion can be applied to statistics. Given enough data and the careful selection of criteria, statistics can be generated supporting any position you want to take. Having said that, evaluate the following question according to your own experience. Are the students of today better prepared to face the world than students were 30, 40, or 50 years ago? Whatever your opinion, we must strive to make the answer, "yes."

More money is not the only remedy for a poorly functioning educational system; the family must be involved. The system must evolve to meet the day's challenges and to have the ability to change with the future. We should learn from and adopt concepts from systems that perform. What percent of students who start college actually graduate? (That depends on how you look at it; I favor a figure of 50%). Must we just accept that? Do we breed mediocrity with tenure? We must give students the chance to fail or accept the least common denominator as the norm. Our country deserves better.

Unions have their place, and have proved their worth in the past. But when they raise the issue of more money for the teachers, the suggestion is met with many objections: (1) it is difficult to fire teachers who are less than mediocre in performance; (2) it is extremely difficult to find a fair way to pay more to teachers with outstanding performance; (3) with the present system, teaching is a haven for those who cannot perform elsewhere. Yet, given the low pay, long hours, and difficult working conditions, it is easy to understand why outstanding individuals leave the educational system early in their careers for better-paying positions in the commercial sector. One result of this is that those best qualified to move on to leadership roles do so elsewhere rather than in the administration of our schools.

The factors that make public education possible in the USA are many: a political environment that not only permits but promotes an education; tax-free state bonds that provide brick and mortar; the teachers, the administration, the school boards, and the curriculum; the children of course, and the family; the taxpayer, where the money comes from.

We are blessed with government that from the very beginning recognized that the future of the country is dependent upon the education of the populace. John Adams wrote, "a memorable change must be made in the system of education and knowledge must become so general as to raise the lower ranks of society nearer to the higher. The education of a nation instead of being confined to a few schools and universities for the instruction of the few, must become the national care and expense for the formation of the many."[4]

But just how does one support an educational system? Just now, when demographics show a slowing of the growth rate of the younger segment of the population, new buildings are not the highest-priority need, but maintenance and improvements must continue. The administration, the curriculum, and the teaching staff

---

[4] McCullough, David, John Adams, p.364.

define the front-line of the battle that goes on every day. Those are the areas where the citizen needs to be involved. Citizens have a say in electing the school board, and must be well informed if they're to do it well. Each state has some form of a policy concerning, and provides guidelines for, different levels of support to its school districts. The degree of efficiency and the cost per student vary from state to state.

Whatever your state, you should contact your representative to learn where to find accurate information on the funding and administration of your local school system. Next, attend talks by lecturers on the subject who visit your town. Finally, consider volunteering as a substitute teacher to see for yourself what the modern classroom is like. After twenty or so sessions as a "sub," you will begin to appreciate the culture of today's classroom.

To make any valid evaluation of the system requires your getting involved in it. And that is a good thing to do. Where to start? You will find in Appendix C forms on which you can enter the names and contact points for elected officials, including those on your school board. Call your school district and the administration will provide you with information. Obtain election dates and see who is next up for election. Write letters to the board, and ask its members' opinions as to the most critical issues at hand. And of course, the pros and cons. If you don't receive a proper answer, get to work and replace them. It will not be easy but it's done all the time by those who care enough.

Contact your state representative and ask what legislation is pending regarding education, and if any touches upon your district. Ask your representative where he gets the information to make decisions. Ask for any Internet info he or she thinks could be of assistance (but don't hesitate to Google on your own!). If you have an area of particular interest, start a file and learn as much as you can. You may be surprised at the number of your acquaintances who have similar concerns.

Contact your children's teachers and ask if there is anything you can do to improve their jobs for them—whether it is intervening with the school board about, say, textbook shortages or even getting your own children to be better prepared for class.

"Where does the money go?" is the real question. In South Carolina, there are issues easy to target, but about which it is difficult to get accurate answers.

1. How much money does the state lottery contribute to local education, and where does it go precisely?
2. How are product-placement funds from soft drink vendors accounted for?
3. What does the state education group do that is not done by the school districts?
4. In administration, computer systems should reduce overhead. Do they?
5. What is the cost per student in my district; in my state?
6. Does money spent on students affect test scores?
7. Does a millage rate increase match student growth rate in your district?

For a source of interest in South Carolina see: scpolicycouncil.com

Regarding the staff of the schools and the entire system, because of the greatly varying makeup of classes, it is difficult to reward the outstanding, and hard to fire the "not so good." That is part of the problem. As a result, we promote mediocrity. Further, the job of actually teaching, that is, of imparting knowledge and teaching skills, can certainly become obscure when one considers all the related tasks accomplished. Let's examine a hypothetical "interview" of an eager prospect.

"Let me see if I've got this job description right. You want me to go into that room with all those kids, and fill their every waking moment with a love for learning. And I am supposed to instill a sense of pride in their ethnicity, modify their disruptive behavior, observe them for signs of abuse, censor their t-shirts and monitor their dress habits. You want me to wage a war on drugs and sexually transmitted diseases, check their backpacks for weapons of mass destruction, and raise their self-esteem. You want me to teach them patriotism, good citizenship, sportsmanship, fair play, how to register to vote, how to balance a checkbook, and how to apply for a job. I am to check their heads for lice, maintain a safe environment, recognize signs of antisocial behavior, offer advice, write letters of recommendation, encourage respect for culture diversity. I'll have to make sure I give the girls and boys in my class equal attention.

"My contract will require me to work on my own time after school, evenings, and weekends to grade papers. Also, at my own expense, I must spend my summer vacations working toward advanced certification and a masters degree. And, on my own time, you want me to attend committee and faculty meetings, PTA meetings, and participate in staff development training. I am to be a paragon of virtue, larger than life, such that my very presence will awe my students into being obedient and respectful of authority. You want me to incorporate technology into the learning experience, monitor web sites, and relate personally with each student. That includes deciding who might be potentially dangerous and/or liable to commit a crime in school. I am to make sure all students pass the mandatory state exams, even those who don't come to school regularly or complete any of their assignments and whose parents will regularly ignore my warnings of their children's poor performance. Plus, I am to make sure that all of the students with handicaps get an equal education regardless of the extent of their mental or physical infirmities. And I am to communicate regularly with the parents by letter, telephone, newsletter and report card.

"All of this I am to do with chalk, a blackboard, a computer, several books, a bulletin board, a big smile, and on a salary not too large."

To add a touch of reality to the above description, here in South Carolina, handicapped children are usually in a separate class; TV, videos, and audio stories are available; and, in high school, teachers usually have two periods reserved for planning. On the other hand, I've failed to mention legal threats and the dangers of normal classroom dissention. For the most part, teachers are dedicated, well organized, and knowledgeable. The libraries that I've visited in South Carolina schools seem efficient and ready to assist inquiring students. Advantage, a statewide publication, is helpful in spreading word about various subjects of interest to the teachers. Further, many local school programs supplement the board-approved curriculum.

As happens with employees in any field, experienced teachers are retiring, or moving on to greener pastures so the pressure to fill positions is stronger than any other experienced in about fifty years. Loving one's job goes a long way, but we cannot continue to trade on teachers' accepting poor working conditions because of a love of the job; eventually we will pay the price in the classroom. Consider: Out of 100,000 graduates with a teaching degree, 40% never formally enter teaching after putting in the required classroom-time in real schools during training; 50% of the remaining 60,000 drop out during their first 5 years in the classroom. This means 30,000, just 30% remain, on average, past the five-year mark. Where the teacher is needed most, in the urban areas, the dropout rate approaches 90%.[5] What was the salary of those responsible for the future of our nation? In South Carolina teachers' average salary is $39, 851 per year. We get what we pay for.[6]

Changing mindsets is a difficult task. It would help considerably if the money already in the system were to be used in a more efficient manner. We know that administrative costs are out of hand when $.75 out of every dollar for education does not reach the classroom.[7]

As an example of the fact that money alone will not solve the problem: the school system of Allendale County, South Carolina,

---

[5] *Threshold*, Spring 2004. [6] See: scpolicycouncil.com

[7] A Different Kind Of Teacher, pp. 26, 29.

tested so poorly the state took over its administration in 1999. Five years later, the same school system has the highest dollar cost per student in the state and its test scores have dropped even lower.[8] In another case, South Carolina was awarded monies to offset costs of the No Child Left Behind policy established by the federal government but not one cent found its way down to the teachers' level. Oddly enough, *state* education administration costs rose: salaries for administration increased by 50%. Since the state already met federal guidelines, the system as a whole required little upgrade. Was that money well spent? An article in Forbes[9] contained further evidence that money alone does not solve the problems. The cost of bussing is discussed also in the article, as are comments by several black leaders implying that the money could be spent in better ways. Largely because of the costs of bussing, in 1991, Kansas City was spending $9412 per student compared to a range of $2900-$5956 in the nearby suburbs. But the test scores of bussed blacks did not improve. It appears when the parents are not in the loop nothing happens.

When the parents are in the loop, programs, both large and small, have increased success. Locally, a program concentrating on after-school activities results in fewer delinquencies, better grades, and a rise in attendance. This seems to reflect some of the results of the KIPP system; when the parents are involved, a better learning experience evolves. In conversations with teachers, I have found that not all schools support the intense teacher training necessary to really make the program succeed.

Home schooling, that is, having a learning program in the home, has a good chance for success because the parents will be deeply committed, and it is well known that dedication can overcome a vast shortage of teaching-aids. If one reads the material published by the home schooling organizations, the costs of following their approach to education appear to be less (see, for example, accelerated-achievement. com). It becomes obvious that a dedicated program, one with parental support, has the better chance for suc-

---

[8] See: scpolicycouncil.com

[9] *Forbes*, Nov 10, 2003, pp. 117-120.

cess. The difficulty is in figuring out how the parents can take time to school their children while trying to make a decent living. There are always exceptions, but I believe that if a well thought out home-schooling program were to have a high-profile success and a large number of people wanted to participate in it, a set of standards could be publicized that would create a further demand beyond our educators' wildest dreams. And that would put the pressure back on the school systems to get their act in high gear.

It's time we reordered educational priorities so that parents and students can see the golden ring and reach for it. This is not easily done as it requires evaluating the way the family is headed and subtly redefining roles in the education of our students so that responsibility and authority are mated. At present, the kids are sent to school, but there are tight restrictions on what the teacher can do to control them. Parents expect the teacher to do their job but, given the litigious environment in which we live, rather than accept that the teacher is in charge, many kids push the envelope and, often, so will their parents. This has led to large numbers of teachers leaving the field in disgust and to many others just becoming passive cogs in the educational machine.

Our legal system is one of the finest in the world, but the continuing evolution of our courts seems to be in need of new direction. The next chapter will open that can of worms.

If you have taken the time to find out who is on your school board and what its members stand for, you are on your way towards being a good citizen.

Chapter Two

And Then There Is the Judiciary

Judges, Lawyers and Juries

Over the years that have passed while I gathered the material for this book, I have become ever more aware of the power that judges, juries, and lawyers have over us citizens. In the pages below I will discuss my ideas on the subject in some detail. But first I want to set the stage with several vignettes. I want to warn the reader from the outset, that the third tale is probably apocryphal. But it is also funny and, in a long and varied life, nothing I have learned about lawyers leads me to believe it couldn't have happened. Or won't.

No.1: The Case That Never Was

Several years ago the son of a friend of mine, let's call him Joe, finds himself in a real predicament.

Joe was a free-lance painter at the time. He left home one day to meet with a contractor for whom he was to provide an on-site quote for the job. But the work was in a part of Houston with which he was not familiar. So, while trying to find the correct address, he stopped a teenage girl on the street to ask for directions. The young woman seemed upset for some reason and they did not communicate well, but he soldiered on and finally reached the meeting place.

That evening, while Joe was retracing his route on the way home, he was pulled over by the police and arrested for the "attempted abduction of a minor with intent to do bodily harm."

Let me paint the scene for you: A typical painter's truck (this one was red), not in the best shape; the driver, in jeans, but neat and clean, stopped to talk with a young girl in a town where the unsolved abduction of a little girl was still headline news.

After Joe drove off in some confusion, the girl stopped the police, told them of the encounter, exaggerating the facts (as teenagers do). Later, while patrolling the area, a policeman saw a red truck and pulled it over. With little debate, and after putting "the fear of God" in Joe, the police arrested him and took him to jail.

Two months later, after the charges were dismissed and the family $40,000 poorer, the district attorney reviewed the facts and the case was thrown out. The problem? The family was required to put up bond. (fee:

$5000), and pay a none-too-ethical lawyer $35,000 in fees to cover expenses through the trial. Since there was no trial, lesser fees should have been negotiated. But very soon after the charges were dismissed the lawyer closed his office and hasn't been seen since. Of course, he issued no refund check before his disappearance.

When the case is broken down into its constituent parts, the facts paint an unflattering picture of just how parts of our society work today. The teenager's mother was going through divorce and the girl's sister had been the victim of a molester. So the girl was striking out against all men when she "upgraded" a misunderstood conversation to an "attempted abduction." She later built up her story to impress others and attract attention.

Acting, no doubt, out of the best of intentions, the arresting officer allowed himself to be taken in by a wild accusation then compounded his error by frightening the devil out of Joe, even accusing the young man of other crimes, before he'd had a chance to check into Joe's version of the story and his background. Of course, it is also possible that the policeman saw an opportunity to advance his own career.

The Press, of course, had a field day, selling fear and papers, because it was more interested in selling newspapers than searching for the truth. Any reporter worth his or her salt would have sensed a potentially great story and dug around for the truth. But investigative reporting is hard work and not many journalists seem to have the inclination for that nowadays.

Conclusions

Fortunately, Joe's family pulled together, and he was spared jail. But not mental anguish and public humiliation. Joe still suffers bouts of debilitating depression from time to time.

As to the family of the teenage girl, well, the poor kid had the bad luck to be born into a family that did not seem, to her, to deserve trust and so she did not confide in her relatives about the bad things going on in her life and around her.

Then there is the judiciary, the legal system. The district attorney did his job but as citizens we cannot permit such abuses to continue. Are we Americans still innocent until proved otherwise?

Joe's misfortune was a result of many trends that are influential in our country, but the most difficult issue he faced - and we face as a nation - is a growing lack of ethics everywhere around us. If we do not as individuals demand a high level of ethical behavior from all those who claim to act on our behalf, there will be many more cases of the kind Joe endured, and some of them will involve relatives of those reading these lines.

No.2: Did He Really Need A Lawyer?

On August 26, 1999, A friend of mine, who we'll call Bill, ventured into a pawnshop. He was pursuing his interest in handguns. Seeing one he liked, he asked to examine it. He was handed the gun, and a few seconds later the gun fired. My friend had a shattered finger and was rushed to the hospital.

That was the beginning of a bitter experience, one that not only affected his business life but shook his faith in men he formerly considered worthy of respect.

His first step was to begin recuperation. With the assistance of his business partner he went through seven months of rehabilitation. The owner of the store assured him not to worry about the medical costs as he was insured, but the medical costs, loss of production time, and the loss of business opportunities soon added up to a significant sum. So Bill hired lawyer one who recommended lawyer two after twenty months of little or no work. This meant that many hours of deposition, testimony and research, the scheduling of a hearing, etc. all were repeated. Time seemed to stretch on with no closure in sight. A fee of 40% of the settlement was agreed upon with lawyer two, and the need to settle quickly was an important part of the understanding. Little money was coming into my friend's business, and he needed to get on with his life.

Although contacting lawyer two was difficult at times, eventually lawyer two indicated that the insurance company was willing to negotiate but wanted to settle after the first of the year, in 2003. The amount discussed was $250,000.00, and that seemed reasonable to Bill who assumed he would receive $150,000.00. (60% of $250,000)

Finally, in September, 2003, the papers were signed. Bill was led to believe that a check would soon be forthcoming but nothing happened. The lawyer was paid, but nothing came to our luckless victim. The months rolled on...November, December. Then January 2004 arrived and still there was no check.

Bill had a friend, a lawyer of course, who volunteered to pursue the matter for him. Well, in May 2004, Bill ultimately received $30,000. Of course lawyer number three will not be free. And then came another surprise: Bill learned that the insurance company had first claim on the settlement from the amount they'd paid Bill's Lawyer number two. Forty percent was subtracted before the insurance company received its money. It gets worse. Lawyer number one sued Bill, claiming that there had been an oral contract with Bill. Of course, it was not to come out of the fee due to lawyer number two. And, of course, lawyer number one was lying. But guess who the judge believed?

Bill? He struggles forward, battered finger and all, looking to work his way out of debt, and hoping he never has to deal with another lawyer. If you learn nothing else from this experience, be sure to read your policies carefully and consult your insurance agent before hiring a lawyer to pursue a claim. Finding a competent, ethical lawyer is not all that easy, but by asking questions of your insurance company you may end up with a list of lawyers who actually perform. Your insurance company can also refer you to those who have pursued their own cases. You may be pleasantly surprised at their results.

No.3: A Lawyer Caught In His Own Smoke And Mirrors

I have been unable to verify the facts of this possibly apocryphal account, but nothing in it contradicts the kinds of things I know or have heard of about lawyers or judges.

A Charlotte, North Carolina lawyer purchased a box of very rare and expensive cigars and insured them against fire and other natural hazards. Within a month, having smoked his entire stockpile, and without yet having made his second premium payment on the policy, the lawyer filed a claim with the insurance company. The lawyer stated the cigars were lost "in a series of small fires." The insurance company refused to pay, citing the obvious reason: that the man had consumed the cigars in the normal fashion.

The suit came to trial, and he won!

In delivering his ruling, the judge agreed with the insurance company that the claim seemed frivolous. Nevertheless, the judge held that the company's insurance policy warranted that the cigars were insurable and guaranteed that the company would insure them against fire, but without defining what was considered to be unacceptable fire. The company was obligated to pay the claim.

Rather than endure a lengthy and costly appeal process, the insurance company accepted the ruling and paid $15,000 to the lawyer for the tragic loss of his rare cigars in the numerous small fires.

After the lawyer cashed the check, the insurance company had him arrested on 24 counts of arson! With his own insurance claim and testimony from the previous case being used against him, the lawyer was convicted of intentionally burning his insured property, and was sentenced to 24 months in jail, and fined $24,000.

To prevent the abuse of power, our forefathers established a system of checks and balances grounded in the constitution. The interpretation of laws was the assignment of the courts with the Supreme Court having the final say. The nation was fortunate to have a man of integrity and foresight, John Marshall, as a chief justice during its formative years because from the outset, the clarification of many legal issues was necessary.

Rulings on bankruptcy, interstate commerce, and even on the supremacy of the Supreme Court were part of John Marshall's legacy. There was in Marshall's day, and continues today, a battle to control the courts politically. Initially, the issue of federal versus states rights was one of the main points of conflict. Today, many of the issues tend to be those of individuals, and whether laws enacted infringe upon their rights. Today, when selecting qualified citizens for judicial office, political parties seem to care that a candidate has ethics and is truly qualified, but they bring more weight to bear if that person supports the philosophy of the party whose candidate he or she will be. Since the candidacy of Judge Bork for the

Supreme Court, the opposition to judicial appointments has been pulling every trick possible to scuttle seemingly well qualified individuals.

It has been said many times that "power corrupts; absolute power corrupts absolutely". Politicians are very susceptible to such corruption, and we must be alert to the consequences of this problem. The desire to control the courts (appointment is a lifetime position in most federal courts) is an extension of the desire of politicians to exert influence for years after they are no longer on the scene. As an example, during the four terms F.D. Roosevelt was president, the Supreme Court was expanded in size, the legislature was controlled by the Democratic party, and many judges were appointed whose philosophy agreed with that of the majority party. Today, the Republicans have a majority, but a thin one, and are attempting to assign judges they believe to agree with the basic tenets of their party's philosophy.

Why is this important to us? Because we live under a constitution that is constantly subject to reinterpretation, and that reinterpretation can be modified by the political pressures of the day. If we do not have qualified and ethical individuals of strong conviction manning our courts, then the spirit of the nation will weaken and we will lack the strength we so admire. Over the long term a balance of appointee philosophies is expected, one reflecting the votes of all our citizens. If any issue is important when selecting your representatives, it is their position on the qualifications of those seeking judicial appointments. It is important to see that candidate representatives commit their stance on that issue in writing.

We have recently witnessed members of the senate attack qualified candidates with abuse and baseless accusations of bias that could only be lodged by those with no ethics of their own. Under the guise of doing the citizens' business, they show no concern for looking badly while falsely accusing nominees of being worse. Is it any wonder that young citizens with integrity frequently choose not to run for public office?

If we continue to elect people with questionable backgrounds, even those with criminal records, we can count on the worst to happen. But then our press is there to protect us by keeping us informed, right? We can expect to hear, read, and see the whole story, right? Nowadays fair play, honesty, and overall integrity will be determined to be "politically correct" (as defined by the media) *only* if these qualities sell newspapers!

There are many issues that should be reviewed and voted on by the public. The two-party system should assist in selecting and targeting the major issues. It would be safe to say the media not only helps to shape opinions, but also that it helps to select the issues we are to be concerned with. That is an extremely important function. At all costs, we must keep our leaders informed of the issues important to us.

The first step in making a decision is to identify and discuss issues of importance. Most politically savvy officials acknowledge that the family is important. However, when considering legislation, both the short and long term effect of a law on the family is usually evaluated only in monetary terms, and then only given a glossing over. The hidden, or unknown, results of the law should concern us most. We need leadership that is concerned about how a bill strengthens the family as a unit. We want pride of accomplishment and honor by example. We want to work with our neighbors, not against them, and we want to know that everyone has a fair shake in our system.

The paragraphs below introduce topics that I believe are worthy of discussion and debate. Each of these points affects the family, some more than others. I hope that readers will find the time to study, research, and form an opinion on these topics and pass the results on to their representatives. Remember, there are always two sides to an issue. We all need to be more informed, and so do our representatives.

Entitlements: We continue to allow our politicians to buy our votes with government handouts. Even when programs are no longer effective, they never seem to be taken off the books (for example, sugar subsidies). The administration of the program goes on and on. Where is the leadership we hear so much about? Entitlements make families more dependent on handouts and less likely to train their children on the importance of being self-sufficient. The merry-go-round must be changed to respond to a different tune. Work gives a person self-esteem and promotes better mental health. We must encourage the work ethic so that people will accept employment that is available to support their family. Should the same standard of living be provided to some through give-aways that others have to earn through employment?

Creativity, flexibility, and guts are necessary to change the direction in which we are headed.

Consider: Every area with unemployment has some sort of priority for public needs. Identify the project, mix dollars available for unemployment with the city's funds, organize the tasks, define the goals, and set a time frame for accomplishing them. Get the job done. Measure the end results. No work, no pay; no excuses. That kind of program takes guts, but it demonstrates a touch of the leadership we need. The issue needs debate, discussion, and action.

Class Action suits: Class action suits are filed to "right a wrong", done to a large, definable class of people. Experience and time have shown that the only people who benefit are the lawyers. There are exceptions of course, but in every case the lawyer is paid a sizable fee. Huge settlements and the consequent large awards to the lawyers give lawyers a powerful incentive to become proficient in the art of filing class action suits. Let's examine case GIC 751725 against Verizon and associates. The lawyers requested $1000 for each named plaintiff and $5,550,000 in fees and costs for the lawyer's effort. Let's see, that's about $55,000 apiece for 100 lawyers, not counting the $1000. Incentive awards for identifying each named plaintiff. An individual's potential award? Nowhere close. This type of case is one step above Greenmail (more on that subject later).

As a demonstration of the greed and avarice such successful lawsuits generate, people have even sued McDonald's, blaming it for their obesity. Large settlements of lawsuits over the smoking and manufacture of cigarettes, the temperature of McDonald's coffee, diseases caused by asbestos, provide the incentive for the continuing pursuit of these potential gold mines for the legal profession.

The cost of these settlements, one at a time, and settled out of court (even though they've done nothing wrong or illegal) eat away at the buying power of the public and the family. This is done often, and because litigation expenses could be huge, corporations' insurers prefer to settle out of court. You should begin to appreciate why we have so many lawyers. Every time I see the movie "African Queen," while Humphrey Bogart is straining to pull the boat through the water, I think of what the legal profession has become. The time has come for the legal profession to evaluate the direction it is heading, and to follow once again the stringent moral and ethical codes we all admired. We need leadership, and we need it badly.

The ethics of advertising: At one time in our history, a lawyer could be disbarred for advertising. It is obvious that lawyers make a tidy sum if their own companies can afford to advertise on TV. Of course, the volume of lawyers, created by the expectation of large salaries, huge bonuses, etc, has given rise to a lot of competition. The qualities of the firms can be judged by their ads. I, for one, am not reassured. Yes, our times are changing and there are fewer and fewer restrictions on almost all activities.

Marriage: Catching the mate of your dreams can be difficult enough. Have we come far enough, matured enough, to consider it necessary to study and discuss the responsibilities of marriage prior to taking that step? We live in a world much of which says, "If it feels good, it must be okay. If it doesn't work out, then we can go our own way."

The rationale for seat belt and helmet laws is the reduction of the cost to society by having fewer major injuries. The cost of a marriage broken, purely because "it doesn't feel good" speaks volumes: little concern for the family, for integrity, for honoring a contract, and the future cost to society. Does such irresponsibility mirror the leadership we elect? I would be the first to recognize that some marriages should be dissolved. None of us is perfect. The pendulum swings back and forth, and just now there are some indications Louisiana's citizens want marriage to be treated with more respect. We shall wait to see if this becomes a more widespread attitude.

Tort reform: Big settlements make headlines and a very few people happy. The results can mean the end of a business, the loss of many jobs, and reputation damaged that took decades of hard work to create. The suing party may be right, but the punishments being handed out by juries have gotten out of hand.

The unseen damages include increased insurance premiums for similar businesses, but, ultimately, the suits result in increased prices. There seems to be only one side to the awards, with juries sold on the idea that companies can afford the expense. Outrageous awards tend to create bitterness in many directions, and keep us from the ultimate goal, working together. In this area there is a real danger that state legislatures will draft "stuffed tiger" laws: all stripes and snarls and no real teeth. Legislators need constant reminders by someone other than the lobbies who benefit from the large awards. The entire system provides temptation in dollar-levels hard to believe.

Millions of dollars have gone to a few. And being good businessmen they want to keep it that way. Awards in the tobacco industry started the money rolling towards legislatures all around the country. Asbestos cases were close behind. Integrity is a difficult value to maintain when millions of dollars are coming your way. To use some of this money to hire lobbyists to persuade others to let the bandwagon gain more steam is something I would call a normal reaction. But our job as citizens is to keep our system of government working, checks and balances in place, to assure the welfare of *all* the people.

I have no objection to a person's earning millions of dollars a year. Professional athletes, movie stars, entertainers, producers, salesmen, and others, all provide a product that benefits millions of people. Inventions, software innovations, new service companies, and manufacturers, all are beneficial. Even the media tries to be informative (needs work though). Their existence supports the well-being of the individual and of the family. Organizations and people in the "legal" business, who promote "something for nothing" as a way of life, either are not aware of how destructive they are to the basic foundation of the family, or they don't care.

Green mail: The art of suing a company for just enough money to be a nuisance so that the case will be settled out of court in order that the victim can avoid the legal aggravation. We consumers ultimately pay the greenmail in the form of increased prices for goods and services. Can the practice be stopped? We should at the least try to force the issues in question to be presented and argued within 30 days with no time extensions. Lawyers are expert in the art of requesting extensions and, on average, the judges do nothing but accommodate the requests. Of course the longer the case drags on, the more fee for the lawyers. Swift justice does not seem to be the order of the day.

Lobbying: One of the rallying cries when our country began was "No taxation without representation." How often do lobbyists represent the voters? I recognize that corporations do pay a lot of taxes, but that is no reason why lobbyists should exert undue influence over our legislators. We vote; corporations do not. Urgent reform is needed to control the exchange of goods and services, for legal support via the lobbyists. If an elected official benefits in any way financially from a lobbyist, directly or indirectly, that official should be subject to severe penalties. In some states the cost of lobbying is subject to being paid for by the taxpayers. South Carolina has authorized lobbying support resulting from judicial requests. Ask your state representative if this is true in your state. Steps have been taken to monitor lobbying, but the process requires constant surveillance if it is to be successful. Lobbying activity should be questioned in general, as we have people whose careers consist solely of peddling influence. This is no new concept of influence, but the potential moral and ethical impacts as well as the resulting degradation of our elected officials should be recognized. We are indeed human, and we do not pray "deliver me from temptation" just to say the words.

Frivolous law suits: I have the impression that "the word" is filtering down to the judges, but they need to be reminded more forcefully that the citizens are watching, and that we want the art of judging to be practiced with better diligence. We search for leaders with the courage of their convictions, and it is proper we want action, "throughput" in courts to accelerate. Support for cases that imply we are not responsible for our own actions should be severely curtailed. The far-reaching implications for the family, and all of us, about the acceptance of responsibility, or lack of it, will be meaningful.

"Shopping" lawsuits: Some states allow a case to be filed in a court known to be friendly to a particular issue, not necessarily where the issue arose. Not only does shopping lawsuits promote larger settlements, but it also creates small but significant problems. It discourages the use of witnesses no longer in the locale, increases legal costs for the defense, and drags the case out. Is the shopping of lawsuits in the best interest of the people? I believe that the practice is not ethical.

Judges: Their qualifications, their selection, and their actual judging. There are always exceptions, but for the most part, those recommended for judicial positions are qualified because of the screening procedures involved. The political hassle in the final appointment of eminently qualified individuals is just embarrassing. However, permitting frivolous suits, and interpretations we witness, are of concern regarding the absence of strong leadership.

Juries: Picking a jury has become so sophisticated that there are lawyers and entire firms that specialize in the art of selection. Houston's system of obtaining potential jurors for screening is one that other municipalities actually study. Their present system provides an ample supply to select from. The problem in most jurisdictions today is that no one wants to serve! If you do feel it's part of your duty as a good citizen, be prepared to waste a lot of time. Lawyers discard those they think have any smarts and don't have any preconceived notions! Fast justice is not the rule, so stand by. To add insult to that injury, the pay for jurors ranges from $5 to $40 a day, according to state. That area definitely needs modernization. Through artful jury selection, lawyers are having a field day playing the public like an organ, and grinding out more fees.

The hidden costs of insurance to all: Although mentioned before, this area of expense needs to be exposed to the public. As a matter of good business practice, all companies, large and small, have some form of insurance to insure the continuation of the enterprise. That is a normal expense, part of overhead, and is factored into prices paid by customers. Companies must compete in several ways: their goods and services must be priced close to or less than similar service, and they must be competitive with other ways of meeting the same needs of the consumer.

When large fines are granted in lawsuits, the exposure to some narrow fields are seen to cause huge increases in insurance premiums. Some doctors have changed areas of practice or retired early due to the increase in the cost of doing business. Due to the potential exposure to a lawsuit, all doctors in a specific field experience an increase in costs, whether or not responsible for a suit. This particular example is quickly reflected in the costs to the public.

Members of boards of directors of larger firms usually are protected by insurance even though they have failed to look after the rights of stockholders. If that protection is not in place, many directors would be elsewhere. Fortunately for the public, the practice is changing and, as a result, boards can be expected to be more involved in the future. Yes, insurance is a cost of business, and it evolves just as the business grows. But, the consumer ends up paying the tab in the long run.

The litigious world of the United States, where 70% plus of the world's lawyers live, impedes many types of business. The efficient use of business time is drastically harmed. As a nation, as judges, as elected officials, we should educate people to understand that suing may indeed be within our rights, but that it is not always the right thing to do. Common sense rather than a pressing need for someone else's wealth, should be encouraged. "Getting something for nothing" should be treated with disdain by all those in position of leadership. That "free lunch" has been paid for with the blood, sweat, and tears of our forefathers, and the bottomless bucket will end up empty if each generation doesn't put its fair share back into it. Remember, "Ask not what your country can do for you, but what you can do for you country."

Do you know where your elected officials stand on these issues?

Chapter Three

The Press Wields a Mighty Sword

Everyone knows that the printed word can be potent and persuasive. What fascinates me is the common acceptance of the written word as being the absolute truth. You can say most anything in print, find something out of context to prove it, and know there will be no rebuttal to the story. If there is a retraction to a front page story, it is generally buried in the middle of the publication. Are the people who run the media at all concerned about their believability? A Gallup poll, *Chicago Tribune* story April 19, 1993 stated that the percentage of believability by the people was 68% in 1972; and dropped further to 21% in 1995 (*Wall Street Journal* poll as reported by the *Atlanta Constitution*, October, 1995). It is easier to accept that the believability factor is even lower today from the comments and stories one reads and hears of, just in the last few weeks and months.

Not long ago, the prestigious *New York Times* fired a reporter for numerous shortcomings, including making up stories. The new paper on the block, *USA Today*, just fired a reporter and the responsible editor, for similar type unrestricted variation of the facts. These two publications rank in the top five in circulation but they are far from the only "top-notch" news sources that have had to fire writers for blatant fabrications over the last several years.

Bias In The Press, a best-selling account by Bernard Goldberg, gave us further, detailed insight into the amount of distortion that appears on what we see on TV. The book was most impressive because it showed the courage we all expect from the media, coming from one of its own. This compares to a doctor giving evidence to prove malpractice against another doctor, or a lawyer testifying against another officer of the court for breaking the law. Despite the writer's blatant disregard for truth, no law was broken, and they had little fear of a prison sentence, no concern for any monetary fine. In fact, some did not even become unemployable in TV. Questions one may ask include: where are the ethics of news executives? With all that power, do the media really practice any self-control? And, as inefficient as it is, our government at least has checks and balances placed upon it. But, who monitors the performance of the media? How do we guarantee their honesty? The first amendment protects the media. Through its judgments, the Supreme Court broadly defines the media's freedom to perform but, except for certain rigidly defined areas (regarding libel and related subjects), there are no teeth to bite the offenders. Thus we have the questions: who is to decide what rules the media are to follow; who should act to protect the public; does the media practice politics without voter knowledge or authority?

But we're getting ahead of the story. Below, by using examples of some memorable events, it is hoped to show how the power of the press, and the media in general, has been used in the past, and how the media has reached their present mode of operation. Regrettably, most of us are mere citizens, not privy to many of the inside goings-on that will continue to affect us.

Before the beginning of our nation, press activity helped to bring about results that were beyond our finest imagination (the creation of these United States). Corrections of wrongs we experienced as a young, growing, exuberant country were more numerous than most of us would like to admit. The press was there. And then there were the ever-present reminders of our rights. We must not neglect the beginning of "Yellow Journalism," i.e., the power of propaganda, and the consolidation of the spoken word into fewer and fewer hands. Finally, by discussing the molding of the thought process of the media, and how the definition of ethics has evolved to our present day, we will bring you back to the leading paragraphs in this section.

In the 1700s, broadly speaking, the media consisted of small newspapers, circulars, pamphlets, and organized debates. There were no radio stations, but gossip at the more popular inns, and traveling vaudeville acts, political stories and the like filled in for them. Topical songs and jokes had their place, and left impressions for a long time. Cartoons making fun of politicians were in vogue.

One of the more effective means of communicating in the early years of our country was the use of flyers and pamphlets. When, during the summer of 1776, John Adams was being criticized for not bringing the issue of independence to a vote, in letters to his wife Abigail, he said the timing was not right. But once the issues of Thomas Paine's Common Sense circulated from person to person, it seemed that, overnight, a fever for independence swept the countryside. Adams seized the moment, and brought the issue to a vote.

We all know the "rest of the story." That episode demonstrated the power of persuasion at its best. The issue was there, the proper people were in place, and the rolling stone of democracy became a boulder of beauty. No wonder the media understands their power to persuade.

And yet there was a different philosophy regarding the press in the days of Washington and Jefferson than today. It has been labeled the libertarian theory. As defined in the dictionary, a libertarian is one who believes in the doctrine of free will, or who advocates full civil liberties. The theory as followed by the press in Jefferson's day accepted any and all opinions, not closely scrutinizing the facts presented, but expecting enough opposition to balance the causes so that the reader would eventually be exposed to the whole story. The friendship between Adams and Jefferson that started in Paris, France, was sorely tested by the rhetoric used by Jefferson's supporters during the later period of Adams' presidency. It was not until the last fifteen years of their lives that they succeeded in overcoming the bitterness created by the writings of John Callender, a supporter of Jefferson[10]

Other factors influencing the times included the Alien and Sedition Act, the number of citizens qualified to vote, and the fact that women could not vote (until 1920). In essence the Sedition Act made it a crime to make "slanderous" and "cruel" statements against the powers that be. At that time there was much concern about spies, and a way was needed to stop their harmful activities. The Patriot Act has similar characteristics, and reasons as to why it was passed. We were not at war when the Sedition Act was passed.

---

[10] McCullough, John Adams, Simon & Schuster (2001), p. 537.

Although we have a much larger voting base now, the percentage of eligible voters that participated in elections was much larger in the 1700s.

The libertarian theory continued for several decades, and in some circles, it is still practiced. As the country became more civilized, more developed, and less like the "wild west", the "social responsibility" theory of journalism began to take hold. The "social responsibility" theory implies that a "hands-off" approach is insufficient as a guideline for the media. This theory may be seen as: The media should accept a responsibility to society, along with the freedom they enjoy, for lack of government interference. That responsibility is to provide a truthful, balanced, and comprehensive account of the news.[11] The Hutchins Commission of 1944-46 was considered by some to be a definitive catalyst for the social responsibility theory. We will return to this point. Meanwhile, let us return to chronology.

During the 1800's, while the country was expanding, it was also coming to grips with the compromises that had been made over slavery. The costs to express an opinion remained minimal using pamphlets and flyers, but newspapers were gaining market share. Opinions on slavery were voiced by the *National Enquirer* of Philadelphia (started in 1836 by Lundy), and the *Liberator* (by Garrison in 1831). The end of the *Liberator* came in 1865 with the North's victory. These papers were well funded by the abolitionists. Uncle Tom's Cabin was featured in several issues, and thus the public became aware of the slavery problem. History does not reveal many pro-slavery publications, and, to its credit, the Confederacy made a conscious effort not to propagandize the War Between the States, and not to influence the *Richmond Examiner*, the *Charleston Mercury*, or the *Mobile Register*. Mixing entertainment and an agenda, or entertainment and information, was just beginning.

Starting in the mid 1800s, advertising became a great source of income for American media. More Americans were able to read. New industries were starting, and famous trademarks were emerg-

[11] Hulteng, John, The Messenger's Motives: Ethical Problems in the News Media. Hulteng is the former Dean of Journalism, University of Oregon.

ing. Some magazines, however, were concerned about fraudulent ads, and made an effort to protect the consumer. The dollars spent were indicative of a fantastic growing economy. The 1850s saw this advertising growth beginning, and hit the $250 million level.[12] Advertising dollars spent by the top 100 companies reached $90.31 billion in 2003.[13] Can we underestimate the power of the advertiser on the media?

The last years of the 1800s saw the best and the worst of journalism at work. Using his father's money, William Randolph Hearst took the *San Francisco Examiner* from 12,000 to 200,000 in daily circulation.[14] Entertainment was Hearst's game, and with resources to buy an excellent staff, and his keen sense of theater, he orchestrated a show the San Franciscans came to love. He was making the news, watching the circulation soar, and loving every minute of it. Being an admirer of Pulitzer, Hearst jumped at the chance to buy the *New York Journal* and compete head on with the *New York World* and Pulitzer. Thus began a battle royal for circulation. The fight became so intense that it would have been hard to detect the application of any "principles of journalism"; but the rise in the circulation of Hearst's papers was easy to see. First was the start of "yellow" journalism with the "Yellow Urchin" cartoon that appeared in the *World*. Then came the granddaddy of all promotions: providing the spark, the tender, and the dynamite to whip the public into a frenzy, Hearst demanded the U.S. get into what was to be known as the Spanish-American War. His timing was exquisite, but his mission and tactics were questionable. Stories of atrocities, of the salacious strip- searching of women, and finally the accusation the Spanish had blown up the battleship *Maine* were all orchestrations of a movement that, Hearst told his readers, only a war would satisfy. The truth? There was so much exaggeration, twisting of tales, and fabrication of events, that the truth was lost in the smoke. National furor created by the syndicated stories coming from New York, from both the *Journal* and the *World*, were lost on Hearst; he saw only that circulation was up to over a million copies a day. Who

---

[12] History of the Mass Media in the US, p. 19 [13] *Advertising Age*, June, 2004.

[17] Streitmatter, Rodger, Mightier Than the Sword: How the News Media Have Shaped America, Westview Press (1998), p. 71.

had the most to gain from that war? Not the Spanish.

About that time there was another area ripe for journalistic exploitation. As is true with many successful new creations, our country had experienced a period of unbridled growth. With little experience to call upon, the result was many forms of harmful corruption. With the support of the energetic Theodore Roosevelt, the media stepped into the fray. Reform had a new name: muckraking.

Robber barons, corruption in government, fraudulent claims made for products, improper food preparation, and horrible working conditions were just a few of the targets the media could, and did, attack. Our country needed to get back on track, and the press answered the call.

The popularity of magazines provided a platform for strong crusaders from which they could have support. Lincoln Steffens became best known for his work exposing political corruption. Trust busting became a goal for S.S. McClure, and he hired Ida Tarbell to get the facts about Standard Oil. She did just that. Eighteen articles later, she had enough material for a book. And all this was just the beginning of trust busting.

Labor's power and corruption of its leaders became a subject Ray Baker took on in the early 1900s. Child labor was Markham's target, and by 1916 he provided impetus for legislation.

The power of advertising reared its ugly head when an officer of a patent medicine manufacturer was caught boasting that his advertising contracts forced magazines and newspapers to oppose legislation hurting his business. Collier's led the battle against patent medicine and, though some time later, laws were passed regulating food and drug manufacturers.[15]

A unique twist in William Randolph Hearst's history was his backing of David Graham Phillips in the quest to identify and rid the senate of its corruption. Phillips did the work. The election of senators by the people and not state legislators was the result of the passing of the constitutional amendment in 1913. Quite an accomplishment. Of course, the circulation rose for Hearst's magazine.[16]

---

[15] *Collier's*, 4 Nov. 1905, "The Patent Medicine Conspiracy against Freedom of the Press".

In the 1920s and 1930s, the Ku Klux Klan was a powerful force in many areas of the country, but its power dwindled as major newspapers attacked it for the bigoted, un-American, hate-mongering group that it was. Of note, the *Memphis Commercial Appeal*, the *Montgomery Advisor*, and the *New York World* led anti-Klan activities along with other media organizations. While initially, reaction to the *World's* first campaign was helpful to the clan, perseverance by it and other papers eventually proved effective.[17]

In Pittsburgh, during November, 1920, an engineer named Frank Conrad, with his own brand of American ingenuity, started radio station KDKA that was the beginning of commercial radio.

Radio was a potent medium in the 1930s. The power it had to persuade was demonstrated by Orson Wells's "War of the Worlds" radio show, which, apparently, led many listeners to believe that the Earth was being invaded by Martians. And then there was Father Charles E. Coughlin, the "Radio Priest." In the 1930s he proved that, even with the wrong agenda, a bit of talent could make the medium a force that politicians had to pay serious attention to. Over the years, Father Coughlin developed a large following. He found controversial issues addictive, and exploited his position. He appeared not to be too concerned about the truth. His main thrust was against the "rich Jews," and he used that position to support Nazism, while at the same time deriding Communism. His change from supporting President F. D. Roosevelt to belittling the president's financial posture as being in step with "the Jews," demonstrated his bigotry. Coughlin's was a true misuse of the media of the kind we must continue to guard against.

Impressions formed early in a young person's life are difficult, if not impossible, to change. To acquiesce to change may require admitting what you learned in the family environment may not all be true. That is a devastating thought by itself. The family has been one of the pillars on which the foundation of our country has been built.

The media, in all its forms, influences us each and every day. If

---

[16] Feller, Crusades, pp. 256, 257.

[17] Streitmatter, Rodger, Mightier Than the Sword: How the News Media Have Shaped America, Westview Press (1998), pp. 103, 121.

we are exposed continuously to: half-truths, misconceptions, and opinionated stories, will we eventually begin to realize what we see and hear is not so true after all? With the advent of blending news and entertainment, we have lost even more integrity. On further thought, a feeling of anxiety, of anguish, develops regarding whether ethics is still an issue with the producers.

But to return to our time line of media history: From the 1930s through the 1950s some great "actors" strode radio's stage, and the news arena provided its fair share: H.V. Kaltenborn, Gabriel Heater, Walter Winchell, Lowell Thomas, Edward R. Murrow. Later, Arthur Godfrey, and Paul Harvey. The 1980s, and later were the times of Rush Limbaugh and many, many others.

But by 1949 a million television sets a year found their way into the homes of Americans, and over the following decade TV's importance to the public would make it dominant in many ways. By the 1960s, television ruled the media. Television: where a picture is worth a thousand words that can make or break a politician's career, became a dynamic force in our country. And what else should we expect of a medium that, even when it was relatively new could take the viewer to the "news" as it was happening...the McCarthy hearings; the assassination of a president; the assassination of the president's purported assassin; the assassination of the president's brother, etc, all in superb detail.

Of course, the *New York Times* and the *Washington Post* were not ready to relinquish their roles as watchdogs. The *Times* did excellent work with, among other things, the Pentagon Papers and the *Post* took its Watergate investigation to the very end. The *Post*'s policy of corroborating information was not followed by all the media. The *Washington Post* should be held in high esteem for its policy.

A little background is necessary for the next point. Using the media, the federal government began a campaign to support World War II. Hollywood, as always, wanted to tell a beautiful story. It did so, through many movies, but without always sticking to the facts.

A few people witnessed this process, thought about it, and learned the power of the media. And they found a new arena to display their talents: The news.

The marriage of entertainment and the news was destined to happen because of the monetary power the combination represented. If you can't make a profit in the media business, you lose your whole purpose of getting a story out to the public. Making the news was the next direction, although not new. The show "60 Minutes" was new, and became the epitome of news entertainment.

Comments taken out of context, answers to questions distorted, all are justified for the purpose of telling the story. Of course the story is the opinion of the producers, or modified to be one that they think will raise ratings. Most likely they are one and the same. Conversations I've had with people who've aired on "60 Minutes" have led me to conclude that we cannot expect the entire story to be told there because it is not news worthy. Yes, television is entertainment.

The right of most media to censor, distort, and tell only half the story is constitutionally protected. Their owners face no penalties, judgements or fines. Libel laws are almost toothless these days. Can we be truly surprised lawyers haven't tackled these pillars of power and wealth?

The Vietnam War proved to be the first war covered in depth by television, not just by the newspaper media. And the Vietnam War marked the second time the media had a decisive impact on a war involving the United States, the first being the starting of the Spanish-American War.

This new power, reporting by television, was dynamic and can be literally, instantaneous. But, like any other story-telling tool, TV brings you to conclusions that are the original opinions of just a few.

Facts and opinions become hard to separate when reporting is subjective. When I read material created during the Vietnam War, it is obvious to me that the media crossed the line, and became bent on ending it. In the heat of a war, surprises, battle reversals, no effective battle plan in action, all add to the frenzy and confusion of the times. The Tet, (New Years) 1968,offensive by the Viet Cong marked the time when the media switched from support of the war to opposing it, describing a battle that the United States lost. Was all lost? Hardly. For the first time the Viet Cong of the North Vietnamese Army was out of its usual jungle environment, and suffered devastating losses rendering most of its units unfit for further combat throughout the rest of the war. Later in 1968 the media showed their true colors by refusing to air the truth about the battle. In one incident, Jack Fern proposed to NBC a three-piece series depicting the Tet Offensive as a failure for the North, but was told, "Tet was already established in the public's mind as a defeat, and therefore it was an American defeat".[18] The public had been sold down the river, along with the veterans of that war.

It seems appropriate here to define the word "propaganda" as noted in the dictionary: "any systematic, widespread dissemination or promotion of particular ideas, doctrine, practices; to further one's own cause." Our media has become a master of the creation and dissemination of propaganda. The problem is, the public has not been told just what cause the media supports or, who is calling the shots. It certainly isn't our elected officials or the people, as the media prides itself on leading the way. Most important, the stance taken by the media is not always factual, truthful, or objectively reported. "The end justifies the means" is a line one hears, and it is difficult not to listen to the cry for the stopping of bloodshed. Concern now mounts when we watch and listen to stories from Iraq.

War. If the press has its way, this nation will never have the stomach for any kind of war. The violence of war has never been pretty, and never will be. The graphics of horror will turn the head and the stomach of any decent man or woman. We are being taught fear, shown the errors of our ways, being prepared to compromise our principles, and to grovel in self-pity. We are being taught that it

---

[18] Streitmatter, Rodger, Mightier Than the Sword: How the News Media Have Shaped America, Westview Press (1998), p. 195.

is better to live in a peaceful world, and let the rest of the world go its own way. Our children are learning from the press and the fare that is dished out on television. We are told we are a nation riddled with crime, with the morals of an alley cat, and living in an environment where we'd better grab what we can, because everyone else is. There is only one side to the news, and that's what we see and hear from our unbiased and truthful media.

Slavery would still be with us if we had no Civil War. Our children would march to the "Horst Wessel Lied" if we hadn't joined our allies during the Second World War. Communism would be our form of government if we had shown no resistance through strength. The Korean War and Vietnam War could be seen as testing our resolve against the Communist world, and our willingness to defend what our leaders thought was of value. Our lack of tolerance for unpleasant conflicts, and our lack of staying power, is a lesson our enemies do not forget. Every chance they get our media remind our enemies that "America has no stomach for a long war." It has been stated that the terrorists were surprised at the coming together of our nation after 9/11. If we believed what we read and see in our media today, it would not be hard to consider that another such attack might get us out of Iraq. Certainly the media would not be responsible in any way for our enemy's believing we would acquiesce to such pressure. If I remember correctly, the Cold War was based upon the fear of retaliation, thus no sane man would consider firing the first shot. The press is playing with fire.

We are at war. Now! To what extent does the media feel it is supporting our national effort? Are they more interested in circulation and audience share? And to what degree are the various news media willing to go to capture market share? Let's review the ethics of our media, and see how far they have come since the beginning of our nation.

Ethics based on the libertarian theory (i.e., a press with virtually no restraints) versus that of the "socially responsible" press (with self-imposed restraints that assure a truthful, balanced, and comprehensive account of a story), revolve around the use and availability of many sources of information. The growth of our nation has seen us advance from the simplicity of a handbill to magnificent computer controlled presses to radio and television and the Internet. From our origin to the early 1900s we had a steady increase in papers and periodicals to reflect the expansion and diversity of our country and our population. Now we are experiencing a consolidation of the control of newspapers, radio and TV stations, and cable networks. We, the consumers of all that information, receive fewer and fewer differences of opinions. The following table shows...

Type of Media	Quant.	Date of Data	Trend	Source
Daily newspapers	1493	1999	Less	Editor&Pub.
Weeklies	6693	2003	Less	Editor&Pub
Television stations	1362	2004	More	FCC
satellite/cable TV	unk/339	2003	Less	NCTA
Radio (AM & FM)	11005	2004	More	FCC
Magazines, various	12448	2000	Less	Gale Dir.P.

Serving over 300 million by 2007, all of these sources of information have one thing in common. They must make a profit to survive to tell their story. Have they lost all concern for the way in which they make a profit? Is there a magazine out there willing to investigate that issue?

The trend of shrinking number of opinions places more pressure on the ethics of our media. Yes, we have a hundred channels of television. It's true that we have cable and many radio stations, but the true test is: how many differences of opinion are reflected in them? One newspaper is now common for a community or city to have. One organization may own the paper, a television station, and a radio station in the same city. Mistakes happen, rewrites are done, headlines are changed with seconds remaining to match space available. As in any complex assembly process, if pieces can be put together improperly, they will be. However, in some cases the motivation of headline writers can be questioned.

We all know that headlines create a mood, but what if the meaning of the underlying story is exactly the opposite of the headline? Not much problem there: as no one person was scandalized, no error correction or retraction will be forthcoming. As the recipients of the news, we should have concern about just how much of the news is "treated" to match the media's perception of what the media believe we should have or want. And what is the value of the information we use to help us assimilate our opinions?

What is difficult to change, or even to suspect, is a policy of slanting the news. However, over a period of time, a pattern and effect can be detected. The initiation of the Spanish-American War and the end of the Vietnam War are two cases that leave no doubt in one's mind that the press had its agenda, and had little concern about ethics or truth. The media used every means available to it to make its case. Propaganda can be seen at its best if the time is taken to review the graphic scenes of war at its worst. Hitler and the Communists were famous for their big- lie techniques. Our press and news coverage? Would the press admit the Tet Offensive was an American victory and not a defeat? Why, if it were to do that we might begin to doubt the "true blue" status of the press, its self-righteous claim to "report the news objectively." Or that the printed word or television news reports may lie.

Under our system of government, controlling distortion in the press is difficult because the major source of concern is the bending of the truth, telling only half the story, and not opening up points of discussion for full investigation. These actions are not illegal. Yes, power does corrupt, and when you have absolute power, what else can you expect but the flaunting disrespect for any need for control.

The subtlety of omission is another major concern. In our own press, the nation's war effort in Iraq is treated as if it is the policy of some foreign government. It seems to me that terrorists should be paying the media to continue its "get out of the war" coverage. It is certainly odd that the only good news we hear is from people returning from Iraq. Why must we rely upon our servicemen, who are in the daily battles, to bring us the good news? Just who controls the stories coming from that part of the world? Is it at all possible there is another side to the atrocities that have allegedly occurred in the prisons? One begins to believe we had better check on where all these journalists got their training, and by whom.

Most of us would certainly like to know how many Iraqis of the female gender are now receiving education, whether there are more hospital beds available, if the electrical power distribution systems are functioning more efficiently, if the police force is developing despite radical resistance, if more oil is flowing per day. And, if any or all of them are happening, how is it all happening under the continuous resistance of a barbaric insurgency? This kind of information is generally found only among families and friends of returning veterans.

Rarely do we hear speculation or in-depth reporting as to whether or how the stabilization of Iraq will change politics in the Middle East. Since the UN has not, then as the world leader the US must control this hotbed of unrest. Whether we like it or not, that has become our position and we had better be prepared to play that role convincingly. How about charging a "fee" for our policing activities? That would probably make too much sense for the media to find it acceptable. Why don't we hear any thoughts of that kind? Simply put, the media doesn't care to report anything that would support our government or our country in time of war. For whatever reason: profit motive; it's not news; we have other important issues, all seem to get in the way. The media are obviously influenced by too few people and these people may not be friends of the average citizen of these United States.

The sword the media wields has two sides. Like a pendulum the sword must swing in two directions to have any power. From books referred to and comments made in this section, one can draw the conclusion that the media have failed in their responsibility, that they have not been proper "gate keepers." The mixing of news and entertainment has failed to meet the test of socially responsible journalism by distorting the facts, by not telling both sides of the story, and by not being comprehensive. Is it appropriate to conclude that the media's use of propaganda does not support the agenda of our elected officials in time of war? Yes, the use of unbridled power can and will come back to haunt when you do not stick to the whole truth. We want the whole truth, so help us God.

If you are aware of these issues and are doing something about them, you are a good citizen.

Chapter Four

Politics USA Style

Politics, like all of life, is in reality a series of decisions and compromises. Would we want to repeat our lives? If nothing else, we learn as we continue, and learn even more from our mistakes.

The political history of these United States is a mirror of our national conscience. We want to do the best that we can to make and keep our country great. Our constitution, copied by many countries, has permitted us to become a republic admired by free men around the world. No other republic has endured for so long a time and remained free to control its own destiny.

I hope that potential pitfalls and mistakes can be seen, and that the knowledge gained through our experience will foster the continued existence of the Republic. In the late 1800s and early 1900s the press acted as the nation's conscience and was at its best in identifying problems and in finding and supporting solutions. The newspapers put us on the right track.

But we must also recognize that the press began to appreciate its power and to apply that power. The advent of radio and television gave "the press" more media in which to apply its trade. This streamlined press, the electronic and print journalism, became the modernized "media". Unlike our governmental structure, these new powers of persuasion have no real checks or balances built into them. The combination of power and no restraints rarely results in public good being done, starting with the loss of ethics.[19] As this watchdog of our political process follows its own course, we begin to experience an unnoticed loss of ethics in the way our government functions.

To add to our concern the media has learned how to support its own viewpoints while suppressing opposing views; "manufactured" stories are appearing (for example, in *USA Today* and *The New York Times*). Mix in a recent poll that found the media to be 87% liberal. Exposed to a biased and uninformed press as before, what should we expect? Problems we should be aware of are not being discussed, exposed, or even placed on the agenda. This chapter will highlight some developments the press should be hashing

---

[19] Hulteng, John, The Messenger's Motives: Ethical Problems in the News Media, Prentice-Hall (1985).

about, that just may not be in the best interest of our country.

Fortunately, we still have the right to offer opposing views. This book is not alone in the effort to point out patterns of behavior that need correction. Our vote decidedly still counts but we need more participation; more accurate information; more public awareness.

We survived the Civil War despite the fact that damage was done to the balance of power between the individual states and the central government. Over time, we have taken a more important role in international circles. The federal government has broadened its responsibilities as would be expected. A major issue that creeps to the forefront more in peacetime, deals with how much of the tax dollars are returned to the individual states.

Our politicians make this subject a real issue at election time, and point with pride to the federal projects bringing revenue to their respective states. This is a real issue, as it means jobs and the flow of dollars through our service-oriented economy. The concept of putting money in our pocket via federal directives is an issue we must think about, long and hard.

For a long time many people have argued the importance a particular presidency or political party has on the economy. Politicians take credit for many things, including healthy economies, but for the most part, the cycles we experience are normal business cycles. Even the fed's control of the interest rate is a reaction to market conditions. When the interest rate is changed, it is hoped that the change will mute major swings. There will always be arguments concerning the over-management of the economy. The strength of our country will always be the family, and the family members' willingness to work, and their desire to get ahead. It may be said that we succeed in spite of our federal government.

What congress can do is spend money. That action is, in reality, a return of our tax dollars. It is regrettable that the efficiency of the government does not always get high marks.

Tom A. Coburn, MD, was a member of the 1994 congress (and

two following sessions), who wrote a book about how Washington really works. It is called Breach of Trust.[20] He addressed many issues we as citizens should be aware of. What was most impressive to me was his concern about the future of our country, and the difficulty in changing our direction. There are many issues we must be aware of, and just one is how we shape our thoughts and opinions. Before addressing the main thrust of Congressman Coburn's book, you will find next an article written Memorial Day of this year that discusses the subject of influencing public opinion. We must accept the fact that the media exercises a very strong influence upon our elected officials. The challenge offered here to the media is to get back on track and look at problems within our government that continue to increase our mammoth debt.

Am I "Smoking Opium", or is the Media?

The results of a campaign may be the only way to judge its effectiveness. The control of our thought process is scary to think about, but dangerous not to be aware of, if it is indeed a conscious effort. A free press may of course take any side it wishes, and have good reason to. That privilege should never be disputed. However, it seems appropriate to ask you to judge and compare how you feel about: Pearl Harbor and 9/11.

In both cases our country was attacked with thousands of Americans being killed. Provocation? The Japanese were threatened by our position in trade agreements to control their ability to expand. The Muslim terrorists? Provoked by our way of life, as nonbelievers, standing in their way to expand their beliefs. Reaction? We must fight to protect ourselves and our liberty, our way of life. And the sixty-four dollar question: can you compare how we sustained our will to fight in the 1940s to today?

The media supported our effort and our leaders in the 1940s, and used its power to persuade to continuously remind us of the threat to our liberty and to be dedicated to the cause of freedom.

Today, we are inundated with stories of atrocities (just as during the Vietnam War) though they are extremely few and in most cases extremely minor), reminded of the deaths of those who are fighting the war (never

---

[20] Coburn, Tom A., Breach of Trust: How Washington Turns Outsiders into Insiders, WND Books (2003).

advertised during WWII), and repeatedly presented with story after story of the same disgusting action in a prison camp.

Support of negotiations to prevent this war, to not go to war against the desire of the United Nations, is ballyhooed as an alternative by former President Clinton. Further, his position is said to have been extremely well supported by the graduation class at Cornell University when Clinton's delivered his address at their graduation exercise. It was the only graduation exercise covered in our local paper that day.

The thrust of the media can and will weaken our resolve, if all it does is present what the media thinks is the proper attitude: get out of Iraq. Just how did the media become 87% liberal? Are the media really in charge?

We hear just enough information to tickle our desire for good news, but it soon gets buried in some obscure section, or is broadcast at a time that is not too popular. Why was it that recently the week of May 25, a speech by President Bush on Iraq was not carried by NBC, CBS, or ABC ?
Yes, the control of our thoughts is indeed precious. Allow me to remind the media that we, the public, do retain some intelligence. Your believability is spiraling downward. People like Rush Limbaugh would not have a leg to stand on if it weren't for the biased approach of so many of you. We must have the other side of the story, whether the bulk of the media cares to publicize it or not.

What bothers me most is one-sided coverage. How can the media continue to be so righteous when they tell only their side of the story? Where are the opinions of those who support our desire to fight for the retention of our way of life? For a life of freedom including the right of free expression? Do you (the media) in your right mind think that radical Muslims will permit you to object to their putting into effect their interpretation of the Quran if they are in control?

The test of this effort by the media is simply put: How do you feel about terrorists now as compared to immediately after 9/11?

Our nation must remain strong financially, and practice sound fiscal policies if it is to be able to respond to unusual economic conditions and enemy threats, and retain our world leadership. A false sense of economic well being induced by irresponsible spending by our government can only lead in one direction. We must honor our position as a world leader, and act accordingly... with a sense of responsibility to keep our own house in order.

Congressman Coburn talked about the budget as if it were a pie. But this was a magical pie, and everyone was going to get a fair share. No matter how much everyone else had "eaten", the last person at the table would get a fine piece of the pie. Congressman Coburn also compared the budget to a family meeting in which everyone agreed to the budget for the year. But after the money was doled out, a sister going to college ran short of funds. Like all loving parents, additional money was sent. But where did it come from? A loan at the bank, perhaps, or money set aside for the last year of college, or the family could address that problem by not buying the new refrigerator that had been planned for as a future purchase.

The federal government does the same thing but with a lot more kick! The annual budget is expanded under emergency measures each year, and spending limits are advanced to next year. What fun it is to spend someone else's money! If necessary, money is borrowed from the social security fund, or the debt is increased another way. In reality, congressional spending limits have become a sham or, worse, a game congress plays to appear fiscally responsible. Former congressman Coburn points out that the underlying culprit is careerism, the desire of incumbent politicians to remain in office.

Add to the mix that it is necessary to recognize that "surplus" budget forecasts are just that: forecasts. A magical door opens to accommodate more spending by congress, as revenue must match projected spending. And the magical door closes.

Each political party has a great desire to take credit for positive economic moves. However, the desire to spend money (helping to assure reelection as well) was projected by some members of congress as the driving force that would eradicate the projected "surplus".[21] These gentlemen proved to be oh so accurate. No one would challenge the projected surplus. Why think of the projects

---

[21] Coburn, Breach of Trust: How Washington Turns Outsiders into Insiders, "Introduction," p. xxix.

that can now be done! The irrefutable proof is our ever-growing deficit. Congress, with their great knowledge of the value of a dollar, has spent our country into a dilemma that would cause a family to give up and throw itself on the mercy of the benevolent government due just to interest coming due.

The debt, our debt, has climbed to a number beyond the scope of any normal citizen to truly comprehend. How can we expect our elected officials to appreciate the responsibility this weight of debt will have on our future, and on our children

Year	National Debt
1995	$4,973,000,000,000.
1996	$5,224,000,000,000
1997	$5,413,000,000,000
1998	$5,526,000,000,000
1999	$5,656,000,000,000
2000	$5,674,000,000,000
2004	$7,133,000,000,000 as of 4/30/2004

Should we panic? There are many reasons not to, but as long as we expect the government to support our every whim we must live with this lack of government responsibility. We must understand why this monster has been created, and deal with it. A very basic rule in solving any problem is, first, to define the problem.

There are those who say as long as our GDP (Gross Domestic Product) remains above the debt we are okay. Those interested in spending our money can and will find some economist to support that view.

Year	National Debt
1995	$7,397,000,000,000
1996	$7,817,000,000,000
1997	$8,304,000,000,000
1998	$8,747,000,000,000

1999	$9,268,000,000,000
2000	$9,817,000,000,000
2004	$11,460,000,000,000 a/o end 1st qtr

In essence these numbers say that as a country, we are producing enough to meet our interest obligations. This keeps our credit with the rest of the world intact. But just how much of your family budget covers interest expense? And what are you saving for a rainy day? And what percentage do you set aside for medical expense? One of the factors contributing to our problem is that we are borrowing more each year, and spending even greater amounts to retain and even increase government support of individuals. Our social security program reflects a growing desire by the electorate for government support. The politicians will never cut benefits; we're always demanding more. If the politicians give us more, well reelect them. If you wanted to stay in office, would you reduce benefits? Present office holders will be dead and gone when the system is projected to go belly-up. Maybe we had better listen up, voice our opinions, and vote.

We really can't blame congress, because it has its hand out too. As long as we expect to get something for nothing, why shouldn't congressmen? Family responsibility for the future is slowly but surely being passed to the federal government. Principles of sound management seem to go out the window when someone fears losing a position of power, or a seat in congress. According to Congressman Coburn, the political machinery has become complex but it is very efficient in disguising the procedures for funding projects in the waning hours while "locking in" the appropriation bill(s). A large percentage of last minute funding decisions is affected by the political process, not by what the country needs. These procedures appear to have more appeal to the professional politicians, giving them final control over spending. Their defense seems to be: "that's the way things have been done for years." Well, let's see...We should vote for our representatives that get the most back to their respec-

[22] Source: bea.gov

tive states. We may or may not have a need, but something is better than nothing.

Stop. The money used probably just raised our debt. The project was nice, but did we really need it? Was the project high on any needs-based priority list? Was it a payoff to obtain a vote for another state project? Was it discussed in public for all America to witness? How long has this congressman been in Washington? Is he (she) in trouble in the next election? Does the voting record of this person support special interests, or the country's best interests? What has he (she) done to slow spending? Can he (she) fight to prevent waste by other Congressmen? Not if the representative is in the pork barrel too.

The need for power, and the payback procedures in place to support it, opens the door for our elected officials; and corruption begins without their realizing it. When people trade votes for power, our country is no longer first in the scheme of things. That is the price we pay when elected officials stay in Washington too long. Compromise and principles are not good bedfellows.

Perhaps George Washington knew more than we gave him credit for when he announced and set the precedent of holding office for only two terms. When a congressman is in office for a prolonged period, and is also a member of the majority party, it's probable that he will have a chance at being chairman of the powerful Ways and Means committee…and for years. Can you doubt the power of that congressman? Seniority controls a vast portion of the activity of congress, even to the point of what bills come out of committee. Men have done many things to achieve such a position, and tossing aside principles for power is nothing new. Rigging the playing field to remain in office seems counter to our founders' intent.

Once elected, our congressmen and senators like to stay around. There are many policies in effect that encourage their reelection, and it seems appropriate to discuss the reasons why there is a 98% incumbency rate.

Holding public office brings with it power and responsibility. The oath of office for all elected members of congress is as follows: "I do solemnly swear that I will support and defend the Constitution of the United States against all enemies, foreign and domestic; that I will bear true faith and allegiance to the same, that I take this obligation freely, without any mental reservation or purpose of evasion; and that I will well and faithfully discharge the duties of the office on which I am about to enter. So help me, God."

This oath is simple, powerful, and should be remembered while reading the paragraphs below.

Former Congressman Coburn pointed out several issues that are important to long-term incumbency but the list grows even larger as one studies the problem.

The privilege of "franking," i.e., free postage, seems innocuous, but even the newest candidates for congress know the power of being able to remind the public again and again of their names. Going through the primaries and then the election itself is made much easier if you can get thousands of pieces of literature to the voters.

A congressman has staff personnel, and authorization to open and maintain offices in his district. That same staff can and is used for mailings of all kinds to the electorate. The time spent being reelected is time away from serving the public. Such costs must be borne by candidates for congress from funds donated by supporters, not by the government. The Congressman's local staff builds political IOUs for him by performing personal services for individuals in the district, as they are expected to do.

Congress provides a video/audio studio for the production of tapes to inform the public of issues before congress. It is free. The same effort paid for by candidates can be as expensive as $20,000 per tape.

Individuals are limited to contributing $2000. By itself, that seems unimportant. However, those in office, are routinely in contact with affluent people, and just the odds alone will assure more contributions of size. Further, contributing to elected officials will definitely appear to be a better investment.

Congressman Coburn came up against one rule which says a congressman cannot earn more than $20,000 per year for work outside that of being a congressman. Dr. Coburn won that battle, but the mere existence of the rule tends to keep citizens with business acumen from running for congress. Further, once elected, the rule makes the congressman more susceptible to becoming dependent on politics as a career. As a result, another set of good intentions bites the dust. The rule has other purposes, but subjective application of the rule demonstrates the continuous use of power politics. We need qualified leaders in congress; not people with watered-down principles. We continue to do things that discourage people of distinction from running for office.

Gerrymandering continues to be a political football. Districts are constructed by the party in power to protect its own officeholders as well as to swing the odds in favor of obtaining additional positions. Minority blocks want influence as well, so they battle to the death over the paths of district lines. Any time different parts of the same street appear in two districts (or more), you know the demographic studies were intense, political, and fought over. The important thing to remember is: districts are designed to insure the reelection of the incumbent. The media doesn't consider gerrymandering a sexy enough issue so one doesn't see or hear much about it.

The art of lobbying has many interesting facets. First, the fact that lobbyist salaries in six figures are common should make one think about the effectiveness of lobbying. Businesses will not pay for an activity if they see no result from it. Secondly, the staff of appropriations committees have an expert understanding of the inner-workings of the budgeting process. For that reason, they make excellent lobbyists once off the government payroll and they've satisfied restrictions on their lobbying (and so do congressmen). Comments by former congressman Coburn imply that it is really doubtful any one person knows the entire workings of the budget process.[23] Third, laws have been passed to prevent bribery of members of congress, but bribery comes in many forms: lavish parties, junkets to study sites of interests, support of favorite charities make up just a few of the temptations our elected officials are faced with. Of course, knowledge of future events in corporations can be translated to sizable profits for congressmen.

Consider

> Congressman A on the FDA Committee; Congressman B on the Transportation Committee. Company X, a construction company, informs Congressman B of a stock opportunity. Company Y, a drug manufacturer, informs Congressman A of a stock opportunity. Congressmen A & B trade info: Companies X & Y receive favorable votes. Congressmen A & B support other legislation for their related districts.

Stock and stock-option holders reap financial rewards. No money passes hands. Everybody's happy, including their constituents in respective districts. How can that be a problem? The problem is that any system that allows such shenanigans has little incentive to control the spending of millions, even billions of dollars by the government. The longer a person is in congress, the more exposure he (she) will receive to this kind of offer. Once compromised, always compromised. Some observers say this is the way things have been done for centuries. Shouldn't we look for another other way to reduce temptation other than praying for it?

Do we expect the net worth of a congressman to decrease during his time in office? Not with the current incumbency pattern and rules of seniority.

One final note: Check to see if the laws of your state actually permit public underwriting of the cost of lobbying. It is permitted in South Carolina.

---

[23] McMullen, Edward T and Varat, Daniel R A Mandate for Leadership, (2003), p. 120.

The successful practice of "pork barrel politics" is probably the most seductive of all methods used by incumbents to assure reelection. On the surface everyone seems to win: The state represented (and some of its voters) receives its share of the big pie; the congressman does his job well in representing his constituents; more jobs are protected and created in the state; and special interests just happen to have their little projects funded from time to time, further assuring donations to the congressman's reelection. And all those wonderful things are done with our tax dollars. It was predicted at the birth of our nation that American voters would learn to vote themselves special favors, which would ultimately result in bankrupting the government. The prevalence of pork barrel politics seems to indicate the prediction was quite accurate, especially when the costs of Social Security, Medicaid, Medicare, and others are included. Unfortunately, we have assumed that a sense of responsibility will motivate our elected officials, that they will look out for the best interests of our country. The pressure to gain reelection and the demand for more goods and services by their constituents means that the country as a whole is frequently last in the line of priorities. When you consider that a large portion of the pork barrel benefits may come from borrowed money rather than from tax revenues, the twist of this wonderful gift may be that we will indeed pay for our "free lunch" through higher taxes. Just how long can we deceive ourselves and sustain our way of life? Is it worthwhile to continue to reelect our congressmen solely on the basis of what they have done for us rather than for the nation?

What do we expect from our politicians? When they run for office, their speeches describe what they can do for us by way of medical, housing and other pertinent issues. "Decrease the debt," or "reduce taxes" are all good purposes. But what about the person? What makes the candidate tick? Does she (he) have a history of living the truth? What kind of a family person is he (she)? Do you know someone personally who can vouch for the candidate?

What was the deciding factor that swayed you to vote the way you did in the last election? Were you impressed by the integrity of the candidate? An overwhelming number of our elected officials started their careers with the best of intentions. However, compromising principles to be an effective congressman soon becomes an on-going issue. Our present scenario for a working congressman includes: living with the seniority system, a desire to be effective, and facing the need to compromise. The combination of those forces eats away at the resolve of even the strongest of men. Limiting the number of terms in office may just be the answer to a congressman's prayer, "And deliver me from temptation." In his book, The Trust Committed To Me, former Congressman Mark Sanford, now Governor of South Carolina, echoes many of the feelings of Dr. Coburn.

Our professional politicians seem to share characteristics with directors sitting on the boards of public companies: they do well in spending someone else's money. As an example, the cost of supporting our House of Representatives has gone from $829 million in 2001, to $1.014 billion in 2004. Total cost of operations is more than *double* that.[24] If you divide the larger number by 441, the cost per congressman equates to over $6 million dollars per year. No wonder we want a return of money to the state! The cost of the senate is less in total dollars, but more per senator. Adding to this tale of wonder is additional money (already included in the $6 million figure) that goes to majority and minority heads, committee heads, and their staffs. The privileges of seniority do not stop there. Ask your congressman what additional benefits he (she) receives when they are vested, and how many years it takes to "vest". It's now 5 years. Add more insult to our intelligence, and ask why they took so long in becoming part of the same Social Security system as the rest of us. It doesn't take a rocket scientist to see why congressmen desire to become reelected. Add a little sugar to the cake: all funds donated to a congressman not utilized for expenditures in running for reelection at one time could be appropriated for the personal use of the congressman when he "retires". Since 1992, congressmen are

[24] Source: www.congress.gov

limited to giving these same funds to their party, another candidate, or a non-profit charity, which can in turn employ the retiring congressman and his family. Congress just can't keep their hands off completely. I raise these issues because, as a good citizen, you should be aware of each and should be asking questions.

By assuming a position of power, the press and the media have abdicated their roles as our conscience. No longer content with reporting the news, concerned more about the "trees" they love than the "forest" we poor citizens live in, the news media no longer provide the information we need to make informed judgments. We, the people, had best realize the truth. We alone are responsible for our fate and our future.

If we continue to have a hands-off attitude towards the political process, we will watch blithely as our freedoms disappear, one by one. Think for a moment. Creating an attitude or holding the position that discussing some subject fully and frankly is politically incorrect is a way to control our process of objecting to the way actions are proceeding in our government. The actions of the American Civil Liberties Union (ACLU) and others have succeeded in narrowing the interpretation of our constitution to exclude the mention of God in almost anything run by the government, whether federal or local. The right to fail is disappearing, and dragging the country down to a lower level of mediocrity. We can't fire anyone, we can't stop congress from spending, we stifle our young with unwieldy educational systems, our legal system is more legal than searching for solutions, much of the information we receive can no longer be considered reliable, and the role of the family unit is being assumed slowly but surely by the federal government. These sentiments should eat at the lining of our stomachs. If we do not show we care by bringing our worries to our elected officials and demanding they take corrective action, then these same trends will continue.

And truly we will have no one to blame but ourselves. We vote less, we don't know what is going on, we do want our "fair" share, and we do not support the integrity that made our country what it was. We need to change that word "was" back to "is". We need a country that is on track to grow and prosper, not in decay from greed, lust for power, or lack of principles. Every time a bill goes through congress that is not in the best interests of our country, we are compromising our children's inheritance.

We encourage dependence; weaken the family... we have become disillusioned with our reckless spending; we weaken our resolve to work for a better life ... we strengthen our central government; separate ourselves from governing the smaller issues... we accept mediocrity; we lose that most precious intangible, our lust for democracy.

Today, we are the greatest and most powerful nation the world has ever seen. We have within our grasp as citizens the power to move forward, or to deteriorate. It is up to us, our neighbors, all of us, to lead this nation, blessed by God, to honor, protect, and plan for a bright, principled future.

It is a simple thing we must do. Honor the golden rule, "Do unto others as you would have them do unto you." Applying this line of thought to our political environment requires knowing what's going on in your neighborhood, your town, your state, your country, your world, and being involved. Now your task is not so simple; you will need to make choices. Strengthen your family first, and through them, work together in the neighborhood. We can start by knowing the facts on issues (even determining the issues), and voting to support your opinions. Easier said than done? True, if we do not unite with others who believe as we do. We should not stand alone. If we talk with our friends and loved ones, as we reach out to discuss matters of concern, we will become informed.

Church and town hall meetings, at work and play, are places where an exchange of ideas can occur. Learning the difference between fact and fiction can be an eye-opening experience. Exposure to family and other conversations, asking questions, reading, watching a little television, all go into the mix of forming opinions. Finding the truth will always be a challenge, but it is a rewarding experience when you do. I submit to you a challenge to devote just 1% of your time in a quest for the truth. That's about 15 minutes a day, or 1.7 hours a week. Will you do that for your family, your country, yourself? As a starting project, find out how limiting the number of terms our congressmen can serve would benefit the system.

When special interest groups contribute large sums of money into campaigns to defeat term-limit agendas and still lose, we know there is a glimmer of light at the end of the tunnel. Our active participation could stem the tide the way the Homeowners-Taxpayer Association (HTA) did in San Antonio. Recently, politicians and special interest groups mounted a campaign to weaken term limits in force there. The $325,000 campaign fund dwarfed the $3000 raised by the HTA, yet the HTA won by a 2:1 margin when the votes were counted.[25] If your congressmen need to be reminded of their responsibilities, it's time we let them know by letters, calls, and our votes.

READ THE POLITICS AND LAW OF TERM LIMITS, PUBLISHED BY CATO INSTITUTE IN 1994, TO OBTAIN THINKING ON BOTH SIDES OF THE TERM-LIMITS ISSUE.

[25] Source: www.termlimits.org, No Uncertain Terms, June, 2004.

Chapter Five

The Keystone of the Republic: The Family

In an arch, the keystone keeps the other stones in place, and allows safe passage through what would otherwise be an unstable structure, providing a gateway mankind can rely upon for a principled future. As our country develops, expands, and takes on international responsibilities, we must protect this keystone, our family, from all enemies, even ourselves, to provide the strongest of all supports for our future endeavors.

As our country has grown and prospered, it has attracted families, and future citizens, from around the world. They come with the hope that they too will find the freedom to follow their dreams. That drive results in a mix of people determined to make a better place for their families and loved ones. Occasionally, when a large mass of such people is caught up in the painful clutches of reality, this kindred of spirit ignites from time to time (9/11), and we are reminded that, as a whole we are stronger than when divided.

Bigotry is a disease of the world, and we in America are not immune. We should expect occasional outbursts of internal struggle, and we will continue to deal with them, using the Constitution as a legal guide and our religious beliefs as a moral compass. It's like being the first kid on the block; you get to say how things should be run on the street. Then new kids come, and then their kids, and the melting pot of America works its magic.

The spirit of defiance against oppression is strong in us, and it is our responsibility to assure all that the freedom of expression remains. But common goals and a common language go hand in hand. To accomplish the blending of mind and spirit, we must not be short-sighted by preventing our children from learning the English language. Accents have been shown to keep us divided, but successful second and third generations of those who have been fully assimilated have proved repeatedly that we gain from each other and that we can bring the best of our family forward. Taking responsibility, being self-supporting, helping each other, those are all traits we admire. No one admires bigotry and, as with whatever other faults we have, we must continue to practice our belief in

God, and work to overcome our weaknesses. Only one man has been perfect, and we should never cease in our desire to continue His way of life. In the Constitution, America has been blessed with a blueprint that permits such an effort.

Despite our faults we still retain open minds. As citizens, we continue to be willing to do what is necessary to defend our rights. We do need to be reminded, at times, to be aware of trends that erode our freedoms and our way of life. The protection of our family, our most precious possession, should always be high on the list of values we honor and preserve.

A humble but interested student of history, I am frequently reminded of a policy used by would-be conquerors and our recent enemies of the past: divide and conquer. Part of the Kremlin's boast was that we would be defeated from within, that we would change our way of thinking, that our society would become ever more Socialist, even Communist, in our lives. We won the cold war, but we should remain alert to a more silent enemy. I took the story that follows from the Internet. It seems appropriate.

Once upon a time, on a farm in Indiana, while a little red hen was scratching about the barnyard, she uncovered quite a few grains of wheat. She called all of her neighbors together and said, "If we plant this wheat, we shall have bread to eat. Who will help me plant it?"

"Not I," said the cow.

"Not I," said the duck.

"Not I," said the pig.

"Not I," said the goose.

"Then I will do it myself," said the little red hen. And so she did. The wheat grew very tall and ripened into golden grain.

"Who will help me reap my wheat?" asked the little red hen.

"Not I," said the duck.

"Out of my classification," said the pig.

"I'd lose my seniority," said the cow.

"I'd lose my unemployment compensation," said the goose.

"Then I will do it myself," said the little red hen, and so she did. At last it came time to bake the bread.

"Who will help me bake the bread?" asked the little red hen.

"That would be overtime for me," said the cow.

"I'd lose my welfare benefits," said the duck.

"I'm a dropout and never learned how," said the pig.

"If I am the only helper, that's discrimination," said the goose.

"Then I will do it myself," said the little red hen. She baked 5 loaves and held them up for all her neighbors to see. Of course they wanted some and each demanded a share. But the little red hen said, "No, I shall eat all 5 loaves."

"Excess profits!" cried the cow.

"Capitalist leech!" screamed the duck.

"I demand equal rights!" yelled the goose.

The pig just grunted in disdain.

They all painted picket signs with the word "unfair" and marched around and around the little red hen, shouting obscenities.

Then a government agent came, saying to the little red hen, "You must not be so greedy." "But I earned the bread, "said the little red hen.

"Exactly," said the agent. "That is what makes our free enterprise system so wonderful. Anyone in the barnyard can earn as much as he wants. But under our modern government regulations, the productive workers must divide the fruits of their labor with those who are not fortunate enough to have such strong motivation."

"You mean the lazy and the idle," said the little red hen. The government agent looked down at her sternly but stood silent. And so they all lived happily ever after, even the little red hen, who smiled and clucked, "I am grateful, for now I truly understand."

But her neighbors became quite disappointed in her. She never again baked bread, because she joined the "party" and got her bread free. And all the barnyard smiled. "Fairness" had been established. Individual initiative had died but nobody noticed; perhaps no one cared so long as there was free bread that the "rich" were paying for.

In order to grow, prosper, and propagate, the family requires nourishment like any other entity. We must feed the family a proper diet so that it has a strong back, proper thoughts so that it is well educated and will preserve our way of life; and a solid moral foundation of knowledge so that it will recognize danger, right from wrong, and the presence of God. And still, we accept differences of opinion. What seems to be missing today are the old fashioned debates and the airing of issues.

A nation such as ours has the benefit of continuous exposure to and input from sources other than those within it. The oriental concern for "losing face," i.e., the embarrassment that attaches to a person or family for embarrassing public acts, is a characteristic Americans could use more of. The independence of our offspring, frequently to a point of disrespect, leads to a lack of respect for any authority. And yet there are children who expect to be respected just because of their mere existence. Our legal system has gone a long way towards arming teenagers with the threat of legal action if they don't get their way. In balance between responsibility and authority, the courts must know to favor the family's interests over those of the state.

This short dissertation on respect, or lack of it, illustrates a trend. Fortunately, it is not the dominant scenario for most of our families. My concern is that we have an effective plan to teach children that they too have responsibilities. The family is where it all begins: education, attitude, ability to communicate, sharing, having a sense of responsibility, participation in community activities, are all part of what is sought to be contained in a meaningful family experience. The beautiful part of a loving family is the serendipity of learning to love.

Watching love stories in movies, or reading a moving story of love at work in a novel, is an experience we all enjoy from time to time. However, some of the television fare we are offered today creates more anger and frustration than fulfillment. Our moral standards need help.

Life continues, with some of us having memories of family life worth repeating. Following is such a story, edited to protect the "innocent," of one such family.

Growing up as the sixth daughter in a family of seven kids has given me a unique perspective and, as some would like you to believe, a slight advantage. My dad used to tell me when pressed to name me as the favorite, "Well, you're one of the top seven." I admit to a wonderful childhood but one that was shared equally by us all.

My mother ran a tight ship. She had to with seven kids and only eight years between the oldest and the youngest. We rarely "pushed the envelope" with Mom. We knew the rules and the consequences. One of my sisters has a famous quote within the family. She blurted it out as she was getting a much-needed "discussion" about the dangers of smoking. She said, "Mom, can't you hit me like other moms?" Mom made sure we understood why. Being the youngest, I must admit to an easier ride. Any "testing of the waters" that had to be done had already been tested by my older siblings. According to me, our home was perfect and we had the best family anyone could ever imagine. I still feel that way today.

We worked together and played together. We were never lonely and never bored. And if we thought for a moment to say we were bored there was always a bathroom to clean. So, we were never bored. We had our own team for "release" [a sort of tag game] which was both good and bad. It was good because we could always find enough kids in the neighborhood to make two teams. But then it was bad because the game would come to an abrupt end when the streetlights came on, the cowbell would resonate, and the (Smiths) would have to go in for the night leaving them short seven players. We were all on the swim team at the community pool, and each summer we kept a routine of swim team practice in the morning, return home to clean the house and weed the rock garden, and then back to the pool until closing time. Now I'm sure it wasn't the same every day, but I sure remember it as if it was. Sometimes we would have swim meets in the afternoon. We would come home after practice, eat lunch, take naps and pick out a favorite Jell-o packet to take with us to eat on the bus. We'd lived in the same house, in the same neighborhood, and we knew all the kids.

On being smart, I thought it was a family trait. It didn't occur to me to be anything else. I think I was born knowing that college was the next step after high school. It was not a choice, it was a given. I have to confess, however, that I was not an avid reader when I was growing up. In fact, reading used to make me really mad. It seemed I was always being told to leave someone else alone because they were reading. My closest sister, Patty, who I did everything with (God Bless her) and with whom I was best friends would actually take a lamp into our closet and read. Five of us girls shared the same bedroom and I guess she was just trying to find a small place for herself. She just installed a special light in her daughter's closet so she could read in there too. You could always find Mom stealing a minute to read a book and we were all amazed at her ability to block out the noise and constant interruptions as we stood just inches away asking her questions over and over again. She definitely taught us the love of reading, which we have all passed on to the next generation.

We had "night cleaning" weekly because, as my mother always said, "Everything just looks cleaner at night with the lights on." Not overhead lights mind you, but lights like the light over the stove and the lamp on the kitchen counter. Today, if you were to walk into any one of our homes at night, you would find the light over the stove and light on the counter on. We all cleaned together because as Mom used to remind us, "It doesn't say Jane Smith on the mailbox it says, The Smiths." Enough said.

Every morning we would wake up to find a new quote on the bathroom mirror. A sort of "Thought for the day" to start us thinking. A few family favorites are" Bloom where you're planted"; "No one can make you feel inferior without your consent"; and "Walk with a purpose." Mom even had my sister paint a quote over the front door. It read, "Happiness is finding someone you like at the front door."

We sat on the covered porch during thunderstorms with kerosene lamps lit and an "open mike" for stories. We took trips to the park to swing on the swings. We went every year to Dad's office picnic at a park where we were all well represented in the age group races and much to Dad's embarrassment very often won. And just so none of us got lost, we all had matching smiley face sweatshirts so Mom could always take a quick count. She also bought us bright pink bathing caps so she could keep track of us at the swimming pool. Some kids would have thought that not cool but we never questioned it and Mom always made it seem so special. We didn't always have the latest gizmo but we didn't need it or miss it. I can remember my Mom telling all of us girls how glad she was to have so many daughters. She always told us how wonderful it was to be tall and how much she enjoyed our company when we were teenagers.

I often tell my friends about coming home from school after track practice to our cat, Suki, curled up next to a fire, stew cooking on the stove, and "Star Trek" on the television. That just says it all for me. My Mom is a great cook and we all have fond memories of meals. Every Christmas Mom and all the kids would take the city bus to town to go shopping. We would get dressed up and go to the Santa Shop that they used to have for the kids to shop for their gifts. After the morning we would go to a restaurant and order chicken ala king and peppermint parfaits. As a result Mom started making the same at home from scratch. As moms will do, she came up with her own, and now we enjoy Mom's chicken stew. It's my daughters' favorite!

Mom is famous for her pies, spaghetti and meatballs, and chocolate chip cookies with her special ingredient. One of my favorite food stories is about her liver. Every Thanksgiving my Dad would get up early to make stuffing. Of course all the hard work had already been done by my Mom earlier, but it was my Dad who would turn on the parades, get a cup of coffee, and begin the task of creating another perfectly stuffed turkey. While he cut just the right amount of onions and sautéed them in just the right amount of butter, added just the right sprinkling of spices, he would mix everything together with the bread crumbs. Mom would use the leftover onions and butter to cook the liver! Now other families would be horrified to think they might have to eat liver, but not us. I still marvel at Mom's clever ways. She actually had us begging for some! She would say." Okay, now this is mine. I am not sharing. I just love this liver and I am going to have it all to myself." Well, that was all it took to have us all clamoring for a bite. I can only speak for myself, but I still call dibs on the liver at Thanksgiving.

They say that you can pick your friends but not your relatives. I am fortunate to have it all. My parents raised seven kids all of whom I have the pleasure of calling my friends. I am honored and privileged to be a "Smith." We didn't have it all but we thought we did. We felt safe, loved, and respected. There was an unspoken code and ethic that we all set out to live up to. I believe it is an attitude set up through high expectations, trust, cooperation, compassion, acceptance, love, and maybe a few well chosen quotes. I am so proud of my family and my greatest wish is that my children experience a childhood as wonderful as my own. It will be my duty and honor to pass all I have experienced and learned about parenting from my parents onto my own children with the hope they will feel as lucky as I do. If I could leave you with one last thought it would be that my childhood did not happen by accident. It was carefully orchestrated by an amazingly strong, loving and passionate mother and father. They never forgot to remind us that they loved us and we rarely left their side without, at the very least, a reminder to "lead with kindness" and "remember to always walk with a purpose."

We could all wish for such a testimonial from our children. Here was a very fortunate family indeed. Family life can indeed be beautiful, but that takes work, cooperation, and respect among all the family's members. The important thing is to produce a new generation of souls who will be givers and not takers.

In many families the teenager may seem to be a problem. The teens are a time when children push the envelope, test just who we and they are. With support from the parent(s) who communicate, and firmly establish the "rules," perhaps that turbulent period could be turned into a more productive learning experience. Let us look at a typical teenager or young student and see their choices of action as assets or liabilities to: themselves, the family, the community, and the country.

To SELF, on a daily basis:

Asset	Liability
When getting up, has a can-do attitude	Feeling defeated already
With a plan of action for the day, tackling first activity, knowing where to end	The day just "happens", doesn't care if a task is finished
When "something different" occurs during the day, ready to try "whatever" comes	Sees no value spending time "here"
Having lunch with respected friends meal is healthy, within family budget	Lunch with trouble-makers, time spent together is a joke or farce
When afternoon comes, prepared	Follows easier way shown, good or bad
Completes today's plan, plans for the next day, recognizes need for assistance	Not caring, not thinking, just getting through the day

Consider the following FAMILY activities:

Asset	Liability
In the AM, as a teenager, you assist by getting up promptly, keeping your space neat without being told, doing chores to assist	Parents spending time waking, prodding picking up after you, constantly bickering with you to get ready for the day
Acting responsible during day, self-sufficient in actions, completes assignments	Calls from school taking your parents from their job, not completing assignments, parents do the work
Not wasting money on unneeded items, aware of family financial status, willing to assist.	Spending time and money to satisfy peer pressures instead of family
Being aware of family goals and striving to support same	(worst case) Knowing goals and doing best to prevent their happening

The teenager and the COMMUNITY:

Asset	Liability
Raising funds, donating time for projects needed in community and in school	Putting down this kind of activity as too "goodie, goodie", not willing to do anything to help someone else
Organizing trash pick-up groups, assisting in cleaning vacant lots in selected neighborhood	Adding to the problem by dropping a "fair share" of trash for someone else
Active in sports, drama, musical groups to "test" what self is "good at", develop talents that may be of use in future	Not trying, not developing any skills
Getting involved with civic activities (city government, learning police functions, theater groups, charitable functions)	Requires local gov. employees to spend time with teenagers on receiving end of services

The teenager and our COUNTRY:

Asset	Liability
Doing well in school to prepare self for a job (reading, writing, math)	Making no effort to learn basic skills
If necessary, part time jobs to support self and family	Receiving government aid via food stamps, etc.
Actively learning how community works	No knowledge of local issues or what officials stand for
Aware of who is in office, and their views	No concern as long as food, clothing, shelter provided
Involved in school military programs, willing to defend country	Not prepared to handle a military job
Striving to be self-sufficient and contributing to wealth of nation	Needs support in all personal areas to exist

Taking the time to talk with our loved ones is not only nice but it's a necessity. By degrees we establish patterns for ourselves and our children in coping with the whims of life. Talking one's way through difficult dilemmas teaches our children that reason is a better solution to a problem than violence or simply throwing up one's hands in despair. Fighting, violence, and law suits are final solutions, not the first. At home we provide a second classroom to educate our children. Educators have learned that an absence of such instruction not only causes students to be less responsive to classroom activity, but parental involvement and support are lacking.

In a perfect world we do not live. How we cope with our personal situations is the reality in which we do live. Our country's strength depends ultimately upon the family, and the capacity of the children produced by the family to carry forward our democracy. In a sense, we let our country down when we weaken the family structure. To truly support our nation we must strive to protect and nurture the family. With this goal in mind it is absolutely necessary to identify positive and negative influences on the health of the family.

During our first one hundred-fifty years tremendous strides

were made in living conditions for the family. Society moved from agrarian to manufacturing, from rural to city living; and with them the ability to spend earnings on other than the bare necessities. During that period movies, then radio, and then television taught us what the "Joneses" had, and helped to foster an unprecedented demand for goods and services here and abroad. The "candy store" was within our reach, and ready credit, creeping inflation, and keeping up with the Jones' made the buying decisions easier. We forgot one thing: fiscal responsibility.

Little restraint was shown by congress, as people continued to emulate the lifestyles they saw in movies and television. And at the same time, the educational system showed little interest in teaching the basic economics of the home to future family members (and future members of congress). Somewhere along the way, by not teaching the extraordinary importance of sound financial practices, we taught by omission that something for nothing is good. Fortunately, we are not all insane, and TV ads directed at families with debt out of control are commonplace. Of course, if everyone was to stop uncontrolled spending at the same time, our services economy would surely tank. One solution? Add a must -pass class in budgeting to the high school curriculum. The active family helps to guide the school boards, and has the opportunity to do something about rampant ignorance of the basic economic facts of life.

A simple thing, high self-esteem. It comes from the satisfaction of a job well done, and it can be applied to anyone in our society. It is one of the forces that inspires us to do the best that we can. But when we continue to provide unnecessary hand-outs to those considered below the poverty line, to classify service jobs as being beneath anyone's dignity to perform, just what are we trying to prove? That working for a living is a no-no? When the entitlement programs make it more worthwhile not to work, we perpetuate poverty. A recent study at Emory University compared reactions of the brain to: being paid for work performed; and to being paid the same amount and not working for it. The study substantiated that work for pay resulted in a gain in the subject's self-esteem, pay-for not working in a decrease.[26] In the real world, to add insult to injury, those who receive the most from the government pay little or no taxes. Living in this country is something to be proud of, and supporting it by paying taxes is part of the price we pay. When you think about it, paying taxes says, "we are paying our share," and adds to our self-esteem. Refunds for not working, at a level below "poverty"? Negative income taxes? Why that sounds like a farmer's getting paid not to plant crops!

The proposals to revamp our taxing structure and consider a "use" tax, flat tax or sales tax versus an income tax, is powerful. Everyone would benefit, and that means so would the family. I take that back; the accountants, tax lawyers, and all the special interest groups whose members make a living from figuring ways around the present tax laws would not. Those particular groups lobby hard to defeat such proposed tax-system restructuring. And they proved to be more effective with our professional politicians than have voters. This is the type of issue our press does not pursue with any vigor, because it (a) doesn't believe that "the little people" really want that kind of change, and (b) because so many in the press are not "little people" and either don't know or remember what it's like to be at the bottom end of the middle class. And, of course, most days tax-code restructuring is difficult to work into a pithy headline. Gotta sell those newspapers!

The "flat" tax contains very strong support for the family. When Steve Forbes ran for president in 1996, his platform included support for the "flat" tax because it would give parents "more time to spend with their children and each other." The entire subject was treated with disdain by CBS.[27] Another damaging case demonstrating that the press thinks it knows what is best for the public, and will say what is necessary (or say nothing) to support its point of view. Lobbying activity by the accounting profession in Washington was the additional force that slowed congressional action. But that

[26] *Neuron*, July, 2002.

[27] Goldberg, Bernard, Bias In The Press, Perennial Currents (2003), p. 175.

does not mean that we should halt our effort to support a "flat" tax if you believe in the concept. A few of the "term limit" congressmen recognize that the issue has validity. It may be that the time has come to try a flat tax to slow or stop some of the inefficient processes of our federal government. As a citizen, if you support this issue, let your thoughts be known. The savings in tax related paperwork alone would save another forest.

Two major problems for families are the lack of energy and time to do everything, and lack of enough money to do it with. It seems only logical that any program that aims to aid those two difficulties deserves close evaluation. The other side of the coin is that the rate of divorce might well be decreased if the time and money issues could be addressed properly.

Clearly, divorce doesn't lend itself to strengthening the family. And single parent homes are more common than we would like to admit. Because of the money burdens on the single parent, that particular status requires even more support if the single- parent families are to provide a proper environment in which to raise competent, well-behaved future citizens. What can we do to decrease the rate of divorced or single-parent families?

There will always be cases in which divorce is the only solution. But today many people get married while already thinking about an "exit strategy" i.e., getting separated. Making a family function and prosper is never easy, and it does require work. Our legal system has adapted to the desire to separate. The stigma attached to divorce has lessened with the passage of time, and as more divorces occur, the acceptance of divorce by the children of divorced parents, is considered "the way life is". Lack of individual responsibility, the urbanization of the population, the lack of embarrassment about divorce in the family, all add to the problem.

It is easy to marry, and difficult to separate. Should we make it more difficult to marry? Should prospective spouses go to class and pass an exam? It is agreed by traditionalists that teaching responsibility is the proper thing to do. Others say that slowing the rate of illegitimate children coming into the world is more important; marriage should be encouraged. One cannot emphasize enough that having children is a responsibility that must be understood, and that parenthood is a lifetime commitment. Divorce does not end the responsibility. The pursuit of matching responsibility and authority of the family will always be important in our society because the family is our key to progress and a free country.

There are no easy answers to our complex social questions. Perpetuation of a welfare condition does not seem to be a good solution. Building up self-esteem has more lasting merit, and appears to create winners for more families. Programs to assist the needy should, instead of being pure hand-outs, generate a list of work projects in their communities. Those living in public housing should be rewarded for keeping their housing well maintained. For those demonstrating a complete lack of concern for the care of their home our system should at some point, must say, "no more." Love of our fellow man also means teaching responsibility for one's actions. The family must overcome its personal ordeals, raising our standards, not lowering them to a level of acceptance found in the late years of Soviet socialism. And we should not forget that the more effort the government contributes, especially to non-citizens, can be seen as relinquishing more of our choices to central government control.

As Christians it is our duty to help the needy. Through our churches we make a difference. The inefficiency of tax dollars and the inability of federal case workers to work as closely with the needy as do local charities should remind us that keeping our money at home results in better support for those in need. Is the federal government taking the place of the church? I see few media studies relating the increase of federal aid to a decrease in charitable donations. Perhaps that's not as bad as it seems; one can just imagine how the pieces would be worded to prove that the federal government is the more effective of the two.

Churches are extensions of the many families that support them. The smaller an organization, the greater the efficiency. City government is more efficient than state government. State government is more efficient than federal. And states can not print money! Somewhere along the way we have convinced ourselves that bigger is better. Bigger corporations, bigger ballparks, bigger houses, bigger cars, bigger government, and bigger handouts. Corporations go bankrupt, ballparks fall down; bigger houses can drain our resources, bigger cars are a nightmare for the conservationists; and bigger government means we all have bigger overhead. In itself, there is nothing wrong with the above list. The American way is to achieve and live life to the fullest. Our system is designed to permit success, but our tax structure is designed to tax those with the money. A very progressive tax rate, that puts the word "suck" in success is "sucking" us into a world of mediocrity. We must recognize that our middle class, the small business, the family business, is the key to our success as a country.

Education has become big business. Our professional politicians have learned that we want a better system. Promising us that they have "the solution", they throw money at the problem, our money, and that helps them to get reelected. The efficiency of the process leaves a lot to be desired. We must demand a better way, and get involved in the process. There are signs of enlightenment, such as home study (the family is the key), KIPP, and reports such as the Baptist Church supporting home study. As citizens we must remain alert and aware of the effect that politicians' proposals will have on the family. We must not accept mediocrity.

Our legal system is the best in the world, but it will not stay that way if we watch apathetically as freedoms are slowly eroded. As this is written, a movement is underway to define the family as one man and one woman. If you passed on your feelings about the proposed constitutional amendment to your representatives in a timely manner, then you were beginning to be a better citizen.

Why did our forefathers include separation of church and state in our Constitution, when it was quite obvious that a vast majority of the founders were Christians? The pilgram movement alone spoke volumes, as this New World represented a place where they could practice their faith without fear of prosecution. The British government made life quite miserable for those whose religion was not that of the "state." Patrick Henry said, "It cannot be emphasized too strongly or too often that this great Nation was founded not by religionists, but by Christians, not a religion, but on the Gospel of Jesus Christ. For that reason alone, people of other faiths have been afforded freedom of worship here." John Adams stated we should be concerned about the interpretation of laws by judges, as they will make the law.

Lawyers, bless 'em, have a great knack for defining every comma, period, and pause as written. What we as good citizens must be alert about is ... the intent of the law. The way bills are written today one needs to be a lawyer just to understand them. Simplicity should be the command of the day. We know lawyers need work, but the structure of bills in congress needs serious study. It is suggested the intent of the law should be contained in the law itself, and in simple language not requiring a legal opinion. Simplicity offers both clarity and brilliance.

Let your thought be known to your representatives. Don't accept excuses. If they answer, "in the interest of expediency..." Ask what percent of the bills they vote on they have read personally, and in full (i.e., did not depend on their staff alone). If you do that, you are beginning to get involved. Pass it along.

We should not have allowed the press to become so powerful, with virtually no checks and balances on it. It might be easier to swallow the press bias if it put our country first, rather than at the bottom. The accuracy and the honesty of the press are a true concern because, consciously or not, it employs many of the same dishonest rhetorical practices used by our recent Nazi and Communist enemies in even mundane reports. Persuasion of the mind with distorted facts was a common practice of Communist media and of the Gestapo propaganda machine. Happily, the success of news programs such as O'Reilly's indicates that we don't buy all the half-truths we are exposed to. There seems to be a sort of a broken trust that we, the public, enjoyed with the media at one time

Telling the truth, and telling both sides of the story just don't seem to be in the cards. The media are more interested in making the news, and molding the attitudes that any position can be seen as "politically incorrect." Destruction of our leadership by using the fear (of less power) seems always to be lurking in the background. The fear becomes palpable whenever the press decides it knows better than elected officials how best to do any job. Concentration of control of the various media (radio, television, newspapers, cable networks, etc) is becoming a serious threat to our ability to our hearing, seeing or reading more than one side to any issue. More important, even determining what the issues are is subject to less discussion if those in control of the media decide to suppress or ignore a particular issue. As an example of this, a good argument can be made that the real case for impeachment against President Clinton was sidetracked by a sexual issue that sold more papers. Can we trust our media? The only thing owners of the media seem to understand is making a profit. If a corporation can be corrupt, so too can the media it controls. But corrupt media can be more dangerous than, say, a corrupt corporation because the media hide behind the freedom of the press. "We can say, do, support, destroy, harass, lie, and on and on if it supports our way of thinking." seems to be the modus operandi of the powerful. How long we tolerate this attitude may be related to how important truth, honor, justice, and the family are to this great country. Remain alert, fellow citizen.

Can one see a crack in the unbroken wall of power of the professional politicians? Will we see more term limit representatives in congress? Each of us as both citizen and interested party, each of us has the right to demand fiscal responsibility from our elected officials. We should remind them that the country comes first, that if we pursue our goals with honesty and integrity, with the family foremost in our thoughts, we will continue as a great nation.

It is very seldom one finds an idea like term limits, something that benefits us, the citizens, helps to insure the future of the country, promotes the integrity of congress, follows a concept that promotes honor as a policy, and requires more of our citizens to become involved. The application of term limits would permit fresh ideas in congress, result in officials less influenced by lobbyists, we would have our representatives voting more on principle and less on seeking longevity in office, striving honestly to balance the budget. This movement is gaining support, and those resisting it are those with the most influence to lose, influence they bought in the past with questionable votes. If you have never voted before, now is the time to really start being a good citizen. Do you think the press will like term limits? Probably not; it just may take some of their power away and give it to the citizens of these United States.

Choices

We begin our lives with hope, dreams, and choices. As we grow, if we are blessed, love is prominent in our lives. As we experience the many hard times of life while we are "growing up," compassion (blended with varying amounts of wisdom) carries us for a while.

Friends, loved ones, merely being with our peers, stimulate each of us to seek and to reach different heights. We each create our own cocoon, made up of our closest friends and our innermost thoughts.

If we are fortunate, we are actually able to use the knowledge around us to better ourselves. But who, alone, can do this?

We need others to help us to be the best that we can be. As parents we do our best to pass on our knowledge, along with the differences between right and wrong, good and bad, and the ability to love. The ingredients we are given for the recipe of life are not always what we want or like, but we can always add to the mix, try to get it just right.

Today, many of us are adding the final ingredients, savoring the results of what we've added thus far, and we are delighted with the taste. We know we can't start anew, but the joy we take in working with what we have is limited only by our imagination.

I, for one, look at the rain as a necessity for growth; the trees as nature's way of painting the landscape; the sun as God's nurturing support. As to my friends and loved ones? They're the final ingredients of life that make it all worth while.

Appendix A

This is a teacher's exam. 1895, from Salina, Kansas. It was taken from the original document on file at the Smokey Valley Genealogical Society and Library, reprinted by the Salina Journal.

Grammar (time: 1 hour)

Give nine rules for the use of Capital Letters.

Name the Parts of Speech and define those that have modifications.

Define Verse, Stanza and Paragraph.

What are the Principal Parts of a verb? Give principal parts of do,lie, lay and run.

Define Case. Illustrate Case.

What is Punctuation? Give rules for principal marks of Punctuation.

Write a composition of about 150 words and show therein that you understand the practical use of the rules of grammar.

Arithmetic (time: 1.25 hours)

Name and define the Fundamental Rules of Arithmetic

A wagon box is 2 ft. deep, 10 ft. long, and 3 ft, wide. How many bushels of wheat will it hold?

If a load of wheat weighs 3942 lbs., what is it worth at 50 cts. Per bushel, deducting 1050 lbs. For tare?

District No. 33 has a valuation of $35,000. What is the necessary levy to carry on a school seven months per month, and have $104 for incidentals?

Find cost of 6720 lbs. Coal @ $6.00 per ton.

Find the interest of $512.60 for 8 months and 18 days at 7%.

Find bank discount on $300 for 90 days (no grace) at 10%

What is the cost of a square farm at $15 per acre, the distance which is 640 rods?

Write a Bank Check, a Promissory Note, and a Receipt.

U.S. History (time: 45 minutes)

Give the epochs into which U.S. History is divided.

Give an account of the discovery of America by Columbus.

Relate the causes and results of the Revolutionary War.

Show the territorial growth of the United States.

Tell what you can of the history of Kansas.

Describe three of the most prominent battles of the Rebellion.
Who were the following: Morse, Whitney, Fulton, Bell, Lincoln, Penn, and Howe?
Name events connected with the following dates: 1607, 1620,1800,1849,1865

Orthography (time: 1 hour)

What is meant by the following: alphabet, phonetic, orthography, etymology, syllabication?
What are elementary sounds? How classified?
What are the following, and give examples of each: trigaph, subvocals, dipthong, cognate letters, linguals?
Give four substitutes for caret 'u'.
Give two rules for spelling words with final 'e'. Name the exceptions under each rule.
Give two uses of silent letters in spelling. Illustrate each.
Define the following prefixes and use in connection with a word: bi, dis, mis, pre, semi, post, non, inter, mono, super.
Mark diacritically and divide into syllables the following, and name the sign that indicates the sound: card, ball, mercy, sir, odd, cell, rise, blood, fare, last.
Use the following correctly in a sentence: cite, site, sight / fane, fain, feign / vane, vain, vein / raze, raise, rays
Write 10 words frequently mispronounced and indicate pronunciation by using diacritical marks and by syllabication.

Geography (time: 1 hour)

What is climate? Upon what does climate depend?
How do you account for the extremes of climate in Kansas?
Of what use are rivers? Of what use is the ocean?
Describe the mountains of North America.
Name and describe the following: Monrovia, Odessa, Denver, Manitoba, Hecla, Yucon, St. Helena, Juan Fernandez, Aspinwall, and Orinoco.
Name and locate the principal trade centers of the U.S.
Name all the republics of Europe and give the capital of each.
Why is the Atlantic Coast colder than the Pacific in the same latitude?
Describe the process by which the water of the ocean returns to the sources of rivers.
Describe the movements of the earth. Give inclination on the earth.

End of Test

Appendix B

On Budgeting Money and Time

Definition

An estimate of how your money and time is to be spent over a given period.

I know a few people who enjoy doing budgets, but they are few and far between. If you take a positive approach, consider the budget as a planning tool. A tool that you control, not the other way around. I find what escapes me most is the proper use of my time. I have found with proper planning of how I spend my money, an amazing event occurs. Time is available to do things I didn't consider before.(And the money to do it with!)

Budgets reflect a lifestyle. It may not be the one we desire, but at least we have a handle on it. We can see where we can twist and turn a wee bit, and stay solvent. Credit cards can spell doom, and should not be considered until you have established a pattern for yourself that you can afford. We are tempted enough as it is.

Take some time to think where you want to be in 10 years. Now you are ready to plot your way there, one year at a time. At the same time, remember to stop and smell the roses on the way.

Once you struggle through your first detailed budget, try it out, and redo it, eventually the task will become sort of second nature to you. Allow me to make some assumptions: (Male or female can do this)

1) This single person has left home to start their first job, or

2) This person is still at home, or

3) This single person considers the military

Suggestions

Before you relocate your personal "stuff", see a banker and establish a contact. Contact a church of your choosing to "see what's going on" See what kind of activities are available to you, near the work place. Is public transportation an option? Are extracurricular activities you like nearby?

Budget line item	Away from home	At home	In service
FOOD			
breakfast			
Lunch	25-35%	5-10%	3-5%
Dinner dine out			
CLOTHING			
new			
Dry cleaning	10%	5%	3-5%
Wash			
SHELTER	25-30%		
rent/purchase			
Utilities gas electric			
Phone/cell	2-4%	5-10%	25-30%
Water			
TV/cable			
Insurance			
TRANSPORTATION			
Car payments			
Insurance			
Gas and oil	30-35%	30-35%	30-35%
Annual maintenance			
Depreciation			
ENTERTAINMENT	3-5%	3-5%	5-10%
SAVINGS	5-7%	40-50%	40-50%

Notes

The actual numbers depend upon the base pay of course.... and the percentages will change as the base pay increases with time.

Can you eliminate a car altogether? Could a "pre-owned" vehicle be satisfactory? It becomes obvious, being single, that it is cheaper living at home. Paying parents an amount of money is a good start on becoming independent; that is a personal and family matter. The military life for a young single adult also has interesting facts to consider. Expenses are lower, college tuition support is available, and training in areas of practical application after military service are there for the taking. (Refer to navy.com and goarmy.com for details.)

Blending a long term and short term plan can generate exciting alternatives. Trying different lifestyles when young can assist in making that final strong commitment the individual wants.

Can you now understand the importance of planning and budgeting before you start your career?

Appendix C: Local Governments

I. City

Council Members	When Elected	Mayor	When elected

City Manager, elected or appointed ______________________

Police Chief, elected or appointed______________________

Call City for information that should be on the internet.

Website: ______________________

II. County

Elected Council | Chairman | Date Elected

Call County Administration for website:

The following are mostly elected, could be appointed.

Administrator

Attorney

Sheriff

Treasurer

Auditor

Clerk

Coroner

Recorder

Judges (some are elected, some appointed)

School Board (staggered terms, normally same length of time in office)

School Board (continued)

____

____

____

____

Superintendent ______________________________

Assistant__________________________________

Your Area Superintendent ________________________

Website: __________________________________

Appendix D: State Government

Governor __________________________________

Lt. Governor ________________________________

Your State Senator __________________ Tel ____________

Your State Rep. _____________________ Tel ____________

State Judges (appointed or elected) ____________________

____

____

____

____

____

Call your State Capitol, or your representative for website:

____

Give yourself a little test, Give yourself a point for knowing the names of each and every official representing you. (11 or 12) depending upon how your councilmen are elected. Add another point for knowing the name of the speaker of the house. More points for naming the cabinet posts. More points for who sits in these posts. And then more points for knowing the line of succession to the presidency in case of disaster.

Just how many of the electorate would score 100%? 60% or 50%? or 20% or 10%!